ADVANCE PRAISE FOR
AVERAGE IS THE NEW AWESOME

"A heartfelt pep talk of a book. A true reminder that when you're feeling average, you might just be extraordinary."

—MEREDITH GOLDSTEIN, author of *Can't Help Myself: Lessons and Confessions from a Modern Advice Columnist*

"Funny and strikingly honest, this book is one you'll hold close and relate to in every way you need to right now. *Average Is the New Awesome* gives you an answer to that restless feeling you carry around with you, telling you that being average doesn't mean you have failed. Being average means you're doing just fine. Samantha Matt's advice, juxtaposed with hilarious personal stories, makes you feel like you're spending the afternoon with a close friend who is setting you straight and changing your life."

—JEN GLANTZ, author of *Always a Bridesmaid (For Hire)* and *When You Least Expect It*

"Samantha Matt nails the unique concoction of concerns that plague almost all of us—and even better, her wise, witty, warm advice offers practical solutions."

—HANNAH ORENSTEIN, author of *Playing with Matches* and *Love at First Like*

"Samantha Matt's *Average Is The New Awesome* has struck a chord with me at exactly the right point in my life. It's clever and relatable—which I guess makes me average. But you know what? After reading Samantha's book, I'm okay with it!"

—CHARLEE FAM, **author of** *Last Train to Babylon*

"A fun and refreshingly honest take on life for the social media generation. Holding yourself up to an impossible standard is so overrated, and Samantha's always (thankfully) quick to remind you of that."

—SARAH SOLOMON, **author of** *Guac Is Extra but So Am I*

AVERAGE IS THE NEW AWESOME

AVERAGE IS THE NEW AWESOME

A MANIFESTO FOR THE REST OF US

SAMANTHA MATT

SEAL PRESS
New York

Seal Press
Hachette Book Group
1290 Avenue of the Americas, New York, NY 10104
www.sealpress.com
@sealpress

Printed in the United States of America
First Edition: January 2020

Published by Seal Press, an imprint of Perseus Books, LLC, a subsidiary of Hachette Book Group, Inc. The Seal Press name and logo is a trademark of the Hachette Book Group.

The Hachette Speakers Bureau provides a wide range of authors for speaking events. To find out more, go to www.hachettespeakersbureau.com or call (866) 376-6591.

The publisher is not responsible for websites (or their content) that are not owned by the publisher.

Print book interior design by Jeff Williams

Library of Congress Cataloging-in-Publication Data
Names: Matt, Samantha, author.
Title: Average is the new awesome: a manifesto for the rest of us / Samantha Matt.
Description: First edition. | New York: Seal Press, 2020.
Identifiers: LCCN 2019016334 (print) | LCCN 2019980848 (ebook) | ISBN 9781580059350 (paperback) | ISBN 9781580059343 (ebook)
Subjects: LCSH: Contentment. | Encouragement. |
United States—Civilization—21st century.
Classification: LCC BJ1533.C7 M38 2020 (print) | LCC BJ1533.C7 (ebook) |
DDC 158.1—dc23
LC record available at https://lccn.loc.gov/2019016334
LC ebook record available at https://lccn.loc.gov/2019980848

ISBNs: 978-1-58005-935-0 (paperback), 978-1-58005-934-3 (ebook)

LSC-C

10 9 8 7 6 5 4 3 2 1

For Grandma and Poppop

CONTENTS

INTRODUCTION

Help Me, I'm Average

My biggest accomplishment as a kid was showing up to dance class.

I'm not kidding.

High atop the white desk in my bedroom stood a shrine of trophies, medals, and ribbons, all awarded to me for simply showing up to class, competitions, and recitals.

"You must be, like, really good at dance," friends would say upon seeing my collage of validation. Often, my mom would ask me *not* to bring friends upstairs to my messy bedroom when they were over, but I had to neglect her wishes. There was no Instagram yet for me to post this glorious sanctuary to, and people needed to know my worth. I was successful! I was victorious! I had been taking dance class for a few years, and I hadn't yet quit!

Sure, these objects gave off the impression that I was an extremely talented dancer, but let's look at the facts. I was on the mid-level dance team at my studio, and I was almost always in the back row for routines. And this wasn't because I was tall. I've been 5'2" since I can remember. It was because I wasn't as good as everyone else. But—I wasn't bad. I made the dance team somehow. I was just . . . *average.*

Average. I was average.

Average weight, meaning my doctor always spoke to me about my BMI being "overweight" and a couple snacks away from "obese."

Average student, meaning my 3.2 high school GPA was good, but nothing worth writing home about.

Average looking, meaning one time in the eighth grade, a guy friend told me, "Some days, you look really pretty, and other days, not so much."

Average relationship history, meaning I had a two-week relationship in the eighth grade, went alone to my junior prom, had someone else's tongue in my mouth for the first time when I was seventeen, and found my first real boyfriend at nineteen.

Average social life, meaning I wasn't part of the high school "in" crowd, by any means, but I did weasel my way into a few house parties, woods gatherings, and parking-lot drinking extravaganzas. Even *Mean Girls* didn't acknowledge the table I sat at during at lunch, which was for girls not defined by being "cool," "nerdy," "athletic," or "sexually active band geeks." We were just a bunch of normal ladies living normal lives eating relatively normal lunches. Except for the year I decided it would be healthy to eat a bagel for lunch every day. Just a bagel. And a bottle of Strawberry Passion Fruitopia from the vending machine. Which did wonders for my BMI, I'm sure.

But I didn't want to be average forever, and I didn't think I would be. After all, I still thought, deep down, that I was special. My grandparents told me this all the time. "You're so special! You're so awesome!" It was a parade of compliments whenever I stepped foot in their house. Even at home, my dad would tell me every day, "You're the prettiest girl in the world!" My mom, however, did not play into any of this. She didn't want to inflate my ego. She didn't want to set me up to be let down. Because of this, I knew what I had to do: get out there and prove to the people who thought I was awesome that I was, and prove to the people who weren't convinced I was special that they were wrong.

And so began a long journey full of trying to find purpose through validation. I worked my ass off for years, until I found myself one day in the throes of adulthood, trophy-less and unsure of whether I would ever get to the places I wanted to go. The places I thought I was supposed to be.

What life did I think I was supposed to be living, though? Well, one that made my parents proud. One that made my peers envious. One that elicited applause in the form of likes and comments online. One in which I could check off all the boxes on the life timeline that society had ingrained in my head.

One day in my late twenties, I took a good look at my life. To me, it still seemed average. Years of school had led me to a good job at a good company, but I wasn't making as much money as I thought I would be, and I wasn't getting the recognition I thought I deserved. I was in a serious, long-term relationship with a good guy, but I wasn't married and getting ready to have kids like I thought I would be at my age. I had friends I saw often but not as much as I thought I would, which made me constantly panic that "everyone is mad at me" and/or that "no one likes me anymore." And, according to my BMI, I was still overweight, just slightly further from the obese side of the equation—but not where I thought I'd be after developing a healthier lifestyle.

But what was so wrong with my life? That I didn't get recognized by *Forbes'* "30 Under 30" as one of the brightest young stars in the world? That I wasn't ready to have kids like I had told myself I would be by this age? That some stupid calculation factoring only weight and height was telling me I looked a certain way when I was actually quite fit, strong, and happy with the way I looked? That I was *average?*

Nothing was wrong with my life. I woke up in the morning, I went to work, I paid bills, I had friends, I had a love life. So fucking what if I wasn't at the adult version of the "top of my class" when it came to these things? So fucking what if people weren't telling me what a great job I was do-ing at life? I was doing good enough. I was doing awesome.

The notion that average is bad is something society has bestowed upon us. We think we're special. We think we're important. And when we don't get remarkable recognition for our talents, we assume we have failed. We have no in-between here. It's sensational success or distressing defeat.

A major part of this is the result of the narcissism ep-idemic, the problem in which people have unreasonably high expectations for their lives. It has been reported that while in the 1950s 12 percent of college students described themselves as important, by the 1980s that number had risen to 80 percent.* Not only do people—and their par-ents—think they are important and deserve only the best, but they simply cannot handle it when they don't appear as impressive as their peers.

Some people go out of their way to make themselves stand out from the crowd by hiding the unexceptional parts of their lives around others and on social media. Many of them become depressed. A study from the University of Pennsylvania found that social media is a cause of this. The researcher wrote, "When you look at other people's lives, particularly on Instagram, it's easy to conclude that everyone

---

* *The Narcissism Epidemic: Living in the Age of Entitlement* by Jean M. Twenge and W. Keith Campbell (New York: Atria, 2009), as cited in Tomas Chamorro-Premuzic, "The Upsides of Being Average," *Psychology Today*, June 2, 2017, https://www.psychologytoday.com/us/blog/mr-personality/201706/the-upsides-being-average.

else's life is cooler or better than yours."* And when people think that *everyone else* is doing better than they are, it is easy to decide they are lower than average, even though they thought they were supposed to be special.

This obsession with obtaining perfection has made people believe that *average* is an insult. That it is something that equates with failure. After all, when people believe they are important, they will be frustrated when the world does not treat them as such.

> Being average doesn't mean you have failed. And it doesn't mean you can't still go after more success. It means you are like everyone else, and that you are doing just fine.

The problem is that people forgot there is a happy medium in life. That there is something in between failure and success. A little something I like to call *average*. And what's so wrong with being those things?

Being average doesn't mean you have failed. It doesn't mean you haven't achieved any success. It doesn't mean you can't still go after more success. It means you are like everyone else, and that you are doing just fine.

If living life were a test, and the teacher scaled the scores, the average would probably be close to a perfect score. That's because most people feel average. And no shit, right? Especially for someone like me who grew up with participation trophies, words of validation, and, later, symbols of validation (hello, social media). When the awards for showing up

---

*University of Pennsylvania. "Social Media Use Increases Depression and Loneliness, Study Finds." *ScienceDaily*. www.sciencedaily.com/releases/2018/11/1811 08164316.htm (accessed May 14, 2019).

stopped, I wondered if I'd failed. When the words of validation became less frequent, I felt discouraged. And when the symbols of validation weren't enough, I deleted the posts. Because validation was not enough anymore. I needed more.

But fuck all of that. Being average is normal. Being average is awesome. And, hi, I'm Sam, and I'm going to explain to you why in this here book.

Consider this book as exactly what it is: a manifesto for the rest of us. A call to embrace average. A call to stop validating your existence through praise. A call to realize it's *okay* if you're not where you thought you'd be in life right now.

Now, this book does not suggest that you throw your dreams away or settle for wherever you are in life. But maybe if you start living life for you (*you* as in the person you are right now, and not the person you were years ago), you'll realize you're *happy* where you are. After all, you're allowed to be happy on the journey to wherever life is taking you next.

THE
I'M OKAY WITH MY CAREER!
AWARD

AVERAGE DOESN'T MEAN UNSUCCESSFUL

... and other thoughts about being mediocre at work and money

An Ode to Dime-a-Dozen Dreams

I stepped out of a yellow cab in the middle of Manhattan. Through the crowds in front of me, I saw the building I was looking for, in all its glory. A skyscraper so tall I couldn't even crank my neck back enough to see the whole thing without pinching a nerve (I've always had the body of an eighty-year-old; it's fine).

Closing my eyes and clenching my fists, I thought to myself, *This is it.* I had a feeling. *I am going to get this job.*

It was a job at a TV studio, the kind of job I'd dreamed of. I made my best *I've got this!* face and headed to the big glass doors.

My confidence wavered as soon as I stepped into the building. Hordes of people walked in front of me in every direction possible, making my walk to the front desk feel like a game of Pac-Man—me being Pac-Man and everyone else being the ghosts.

I started to wonder if this place was for me. By no means was I a small-town girl, but maybe I was a small-company girl. I had never been in such a big office before, with multiple sections of elevators organized by floors, each with its own security guard to check badges. My job experience thus far had consisted of four internships at small- to medium-sized offices. I had known or at least recognized most people in those offices every day, and people had known and recognized me. Was a gigantic place like this the best thing for me? Would this place eat me alive?

Eventually, I made my way through the elevator chambers, up to the office where my interview would be held. While I waited in the smartly appointed lounge, an employee came by, and we chatted a bit. After making small talk, I asked how long he'd been at the company.

His response: "Oh, I've been working here since I was in the company's post-graduate program. I'm not sure if you're familiar with it. I'm actually surprised they're interviewing outside candidates and not just hiring someone directly from that program. You're lucky."

My heart sunk.

I'd applied to that program—and I was rejected. I began to think, if I was too mediocre to get accepted into that program, why would I get offered this job? Panic set in as I wondered what I was even doing there in the first place.

Had I set the bar too high for my average self?

Were my dreams not realistic for someone as ordinary as myself?

Is that why they called them dreams—because they weren't meant to happen in real life?

The interview happened. The executive asked questions. I answered them. It all went perfectly fine. And then I went home.

No surprise, I didn't get the job. A few weeks later, I woke up to an email from the company's HR department. Like I did when I had arrived at the office on that chilly November day, I closed my eyes, clenched my fists, and thought to myself, *This is it.* I then clicked on the email, and there it was: the rejection I didn't know I had been waiting for.

At first, I blamed myself. What if I'd been more impressive? Listed more internships on my resume? Been more willing to work for practically nothing?

If I wasn't so goddamn ordinary, would I have gotten the job?

But then I realized—this was not my fault.

I didn't get rejected because I was unimpressive. I got rejected because someone else was more impressive than I was. And being average wasn't keeping me from my dreams.

It was keeping me on track to go after my dreams—to pursue, and eventually achieve, what was meant to be.

Even though I didn't get that particular job, I knew I was still allowed to have the dream. I also knew it didn't mean I would be a horrible human if that dream never became a reality for me. At the very least, I was proud of actually getting that interview. No, I might not have gotten the job, but I was good enough, and I knew eventually someone would take a chance on average me.

But wait! That's not where the story ends.

> Being average wasn't keeping me from my dreams. It was keeping me on track to go after my dreams—to pursue, and eventually achieve, what was meant to be.

After a few years of working toward my dream of a career in television, I was doing exactly that: working in television! But—I wasn't happy. I had achieved my dream, but it didn't feel like it. The work wasn't all that interesting, and the people didn't make me want to rush to the office every morning, either. So, what was wrong?

I began to wonder why I was so focused on achieving this dream in the first place. Was it so I could prove my exceptionalism to people? Was it so I could showcase an impressive lifestyle? Was it so I could climb to "above average" status before my average peers? Whatever the case, this dream was not working out for me, and I needed to accept that.

For too long, I tried to stand out and prove that I wasn't average by putting pressure on myself to achieve dreams by certain times. I feared that being ordinary was hurting me in the job market and would continue to be a burden in my career if I did not prove myself immediately. What I should have been doing instead, though, was embracing my average-ness and figuring shit out along the way to finding happiness.

———

LUCKILY, AS ANY average person does, I had other dreams. Along with owning a summer oceanfront home in Cape Cod, having abs without having to work for them, and teleporting, I also dreamed of becoming a writer.

I had always loved writing. Was I good at writing? I wasn't sure. I wasn't a prodigy. I was an average girl with average grades from an average suburban town with an average talent for writing papers on the No Fear Shakespeare books—you know, the ones where they translate his plays into modern English. How could someone as average as me go after the dream of becoming a writer?

When my dream of working in television didn't work out, I said fuck it and started chasing my dream of writing. I knew I might be average at it, and I knew I had a lot to learn. And I knew success—whatever that looked like— wouldn't happen overnight, if it was to happen at all. This was a dream, after all! Not all dreams are meant to happen. That's why they are dreams. But because I was able to embrace the fact that I was ordinary, it made me work that much harder at my dream, and eventually I really did become a writer.

Average people are allowed to have dreams. We're allowed to dream big, small, and medium-sized. We're allowed to chase dreams, fail at dreams, and succeed at dreams. What we need to remember is that our worth is not defined by whether we achieve a dream. Our worth is defined by how happy we are while going after them. After all, without our dime-a-dozen dreams, we would have nothing in life to strive for. In that case, wouldn't you prefer chasing dreams over succeeding at all of them, anyway? I know I would. Without my average dreams, I have nothing.

15 Things Ordinary People Embrace About the Working World

1. As mediocre people, we never take a job offer for granted.

Dozens, sometimes hundreds, sometimes thousands of people apply to job listings. Job listings for which only one lucky person can receive the golden ticket. With resumes that are great but ordinary when compared to the other applicants, it can be a hard gig out there for average job applicants. Whenever you start to go down the dark path of hating your job (similar to how I often go down dark paths of hating all the clothes in my closet), just remember that your job chose you. Yes, average *you* out of all the other people out there. They could have chosen someone else, but they didn't (which is great for me because with my job, I can always afford new clothes to replace the ones I randomly start to hate).

2. It's perfectly normal to not get praised on the regular.

As children, many of us grew up hearing "You're awesome!" after doing literally nothing worthy of praise and received trophies for simply participating in activities. Then, we got to the workplace, where no one applauds us for completing tasks, such as promptly responding to emails, hitting goals, and altogether doing the things listed in our job description. But why would we be praised for those things? We are literally doing what we're supposed to be doing. If you ever find yourself down about the lack of recognition you're getting at work, just remind yourself this is a good thing. If you're not doing a good enough job, you're going to hear about it—and it won't be good at all. This is why average really is awesome in the workplace.

3. Sometimes it's better to be good than great.

We're not all going to be the best in our fields, and that's okay. There's only room for so many people at the top. You can still be a good lawyer, engineer, nurse, salesperson, marketer, or whatever occupation you are in without being on a list of the most impressive ones out there. It can be hard to remember this when you get zero praise at work and see top-notch employees publicly getting all the praise, but with great honor comes great expectations. Would you rather be held to a higher standard and be condemned for doing a good job, or would you rather be consistently good and lauded when you do great? Personally, I'm good with being good.

4. We don't have to be exceptional to trust our instincts.

I used to always ask if it was okay to do certain things at work before doing them. I knew I was just okay at my job, and I got nervous about every little decision I needed to make. That is, until someone told me, "It's easier to ask for forgiveness than permission." After this, I began to trust my gut and started doing what I thought was right instead of annoying my boss every five seconds to find out. And guess what? I've been wrong many times, but I've never had to ask for forgiveness . . . at least not yet. Not to mention, those mistakes taught me more than I would have learned if I didn't make them.

5. A good-enough attitude goes a long way.

You don't have to be overly friendly to everyone and smile all the time, but you certainly should never be a dick, either. Maintaining that happy-medium attitude is essential in order for average people to excel at work. Mediocre people are replaceable, so if your attitude is shit, guess where you're going?

6. *Sometimes it's best to aim for the happy medium.*

When it comes down to it, work is just *work* for everyday employees. It's not our lives—or at least it shouldn't be. It's just where we go for approximately forty hours a week and how we make money. Thus, as an average employee, you should never lose your shit over things that piss you off at work. You should either speak up with solutions of how things could be changed for the better, or forget it and move on. Complaining never makes a situation better.

7. *It's okay to keep our work relationships
on par with our job performance.*

You don't have to be best friends with your coworkers. Hell, you don't need to even be friends with them. But to remain an average employee with a good enough attitude, you have to attend a healthy mix of "work things." Whether it's getting coffee together during the day or grabbing drinks at the bar around the corner at the end of the day, it's important to bond with coworkers outside of the office. I know. Going places other than home after work is hard, especially when you have to go somewhere that involves the people you were just with all day, but you can't always skip it. Go. Be social. Meet the people your coworkers are when they're not in the office. It won't hurt. In fact, it might make work easier when you find out everyone else is pretty unexceptional and ordinary, too.

8. Not taking all of our paid time off doesn't make us more impressive.

If you are average at your job, going into the office more than you are supposed to isn't going to change anything. You're not a hero for working so much that you accidentally missed out on your allotted vacation days. Nor are you exceptional for working while supposedly taking those days off. Average people need time off—for being sick, for mental health, for family time, for just because. Unless you own your own business and have no one covering for you, as a mediocre person, you're not that important. Stop pretending and go live your life. You'll be happier, I promise!

9. Average people should help average people— we need each other.

Average people lift other average people up. Literally. There are only so many positions at a company. Because of this, you may see an average coworker who is a lot like you and think, *I must do better than them in order to grow.* But that's not how it should be. If you work together, you can learn from each other as you climb the ladder together. Sure, you may be at different heights at some points, but that's okay. It's bound to happen, anyway. Wouldn't you rather have a fellow average coworker who will reach down and help you up than have to climb alone?

10. No one expects us to be impressive at networking events anyway, so we might as well fucking talk to people.

Never have I ever left a networking event and been like YES, I am so proud of myself for awkwardly standing in the corner and nibbling on a piece of cheese with a glass of wine in my hand, continuously asking my friend, "Should we go up to anyone?" Well, self, yes, you should go up to people. That is the fucking point of networking events. It won't be weird. Average people are the target demographic of these things. Impressive people are too busy living their extraordinary lives to have time for such events, unless they're speaking at them or being paid to go. Ordinary commoners like us, though? We need to network and meet likeminded, everyday people. So don't worry that no one will want to talk to you. Everyone there signed up for the awkwardness. Embrace it and try to talk to a stranger. You never know whom you'll meet, and like I said before, average people lift other average people up. You could always use more of them in your life.

11. Average does not mean forgettable.

One of the worst things average people can do is not keep in touch with old coworkers because they assume everyone forgot about them. No matter how unexceptional you are, keeping in touch is really what makes you memorable.

12. *Rejection can keep us in check—in a good way.*

When you're average, rejection is hardly ever about you. It's about someone else being better suited for whatever it is you were going for. It's not that you weren't good enough. You *were* good enough. That's why you were in the running. It's that there's something better suited for you out there. If you keep getting rejected on your quest to find it, you know it's okay, because, well, you're just like everyone else. You're an average person up against a bunch of average people. You'll find what you need eventually, as long as you don't give up.

13. *It's okay to do things we love even if we know we're pretty unimpressive at them.*

This one is a case-by-case situation. Like, you probably shouldn't be a surgeon if you're not great at performing surgery, but I feel like things like that should be self-explanatory to ordinary people. This is more if you enjoy something like writing, you should fucking write and keep at your passion so you can get better at it. If you love trying to start companies, you should keep inventing shit, even if your big ideas go nowhere. You should never let fear of not being good at it keep you from trying a new profession or learning a new skill at work. Embrace your average-ness and stop expecting everything to be easy and perfect. You can't become good at something without working at it, after all.

14. We should always be honest about our value.

You don't have to be super impressive to ask for more at work. You just have to be good enough at what you do, and know that while you know stuff, there is always more for you to learn. There is always more for everyone to learn. No one knows everything. Not even the people who seem like they do. *Especially* the people who seem like they do. If you can own your mediocrity and be humble, while remaining eager to work hard and learn, it will take you far, no exceptionalism needed.

15. Nothing is more important than being happy with what we have.

While we commoners aren't landing on any prestigious lists of accomplished humans or winning awards for being exemplary employees, we are still accomplishing things in our own right. The pure act of being offered a job is a feat in itself. Whether it's a promotion or a simple "thank you" note from a manager for something random, take all of it in stride. Just because you celebrate the small shit doesn't mean you have to forego your greater goals. Average people should always remain ambitious. It's what keeps us going. We just can't forget to applaud all of our average (and awesome!) accomplishments along the way.

It's Okay If You Don't Love What You Do

One of the worst platitudes ever is, "If you love what you do, you'll never work a day in your life." Seriously, that nonsense is full of lies and false hope, and if you believe it, your average world may one day get rocked when you discover that work will always be work any time it is in fact work.

Let's discuss.

Getting paid is pretty great.

Work is getting paid to do something for someone else. Whether that's an employer, a client, or an investor, or you work for yourself or for a business, you need feedback from others to survive. After all, you can't get paid by yourself. Not even Beyoncé can get paid by herself.

Because of this, you're going to have to deal with the opinions of other people. You might not love everything that happens during your working process, and you might not love the way your work looks in the end, but this is how it is.

This is the case for basically every single work scenario I can think of, including my own. Let's take a look at the things I love: my husband, my family, my friends, my bed, my couch, Pure Barre, french fries, pizza, Target, overpriced coffees, llamas, oh, and writing. Yes, I love writing.

One may assume that because writing is on the list of things I love, that I must fucking love any job I do that includes writing. However, when you're being paid to do things, there's a 95 percent chance that stuff is not going to be *exactly* what you want to do. For example, I may love writing about pigeons (I don't, this a hypothetical situation, and a pigeon is the first thing that came to mind, what the actual fuck), but if I am getting paid to write about pigeons, I am probably going to have to write about pigeons in a certain way that is different from what I would have loved to do.

The same goes for other occupations. If you love making art, but you want to get paid for it, you need to consider what other people love and want, not just what you love and want. If you love being a lawyer, you don't need to love all of your clients or all of the cases you work on. If you love working for yourself, you don't need to love every project you take on.

Exceptional people may have it different than us commoners when it comes to loving the shit they're getting paid to do. Let's take Beyoncé, for example, again. She is literally so exceptional that people pay her to do whatever the fuck she wants to do. Okay, I don't know this for a fact. I'm just assuming. In actuality, I'm sure even Beyoncé gets asked to do things differently by the people who are paying her to do it. Just, you know, not as much as we would be asked. "We" being the general public that is not Beyoncé.

There are also CEOs and executives of major companies. You might think these above-average people have it all figured out, but one could argue that with more responsibilities comes more stress. Not only do they have to deal with people's differing opinions and a shit ton of stress on a regular basis, but they also have to make their company stay afloat! This is one area where I'd personally rather be average, because there's a better chance you can do more of what you love when your every move does not impact a bunch of other people.

It's okay to have mixed feelings about your work.

While I've already explained you don't have to always love the physical work you're doing, you also don't have to always love all the other shit that comes along with it.

The verb *work* embodies so much more than the actual, physical work you are producing. It's also about the people you have to work with. It involves the stress of getting things done. It involves the anxiety of making things right.

Just because work might make you angry, frustrated, tired, sad, or any other emotion that isn't "delighted," that doesn't mean you don't enjoy what you're doing or that you're doing a bad job at life. It means you're an average human working an average job.

Once upon a time, I stumbled upon a side hustle: writing for the internet. I fell in love. But as soon as I started making some money from it, that feeling of love became more intermittent. If I wanted the money to keep coming in, I had to write certain things based on what I knew people would love instead of on what I actually loved, and I had to work on the gig a certain number of hours a week to maintain it, even if I was tired and busy. What started as a fun side activity quickly became the root of occasional stress and the cause of exhaustion. It's not to say I didn't still love parts of what I was doing. I did. But the honeymoon phase was over. I wasn't head-over-heels infatuated. I loved what I was doing some of the time, liked what I was doing most of the time, and disliked what I was doing a small amount of the time.

I like to believe that my side-hustle scenario is the closest I will get to being happy with what I do. I found the happy medium of hustling. I truly enjoyed what I was doing. I was no longer overhyped about it, and sometimes it stressed me out, but I didn't completely hate it. I did really, actually like it. Which brings me to my next point . . .

It's perfectly fine to like—rather than love— what you're doing.

In fact, in some cases, it can be better.

When you're not crazily passionate about something, and someone who is paying you asks you to do something, you're less likely to care that you disagree with them. You're less likely to blow the whole thing out of proportion, get stressed, catch feelings, and move to the other side of the spectrum such that you now hate what you're doing. When you *like* what you do, you're in the happy medium of things. You don't get impacted by shit like this.

This is why ordinary jobs rock. You enjoy what you're doing, but you're open to feedback and other people's opinions. Your life wouldn't be over if you stopped doing it, but you also don't complain about "needing a job" ever. You're just . . . fine. Everything is . . . fine. And guess what? When it comes to work, that's good. No, that's great. That's awesome.

In conclusion: good enough is good enough.

My final request to my fellow average people: can you please stop lying to yourself and stop buying home décor that broadcasts messages like "If you love what you do, you'll never work a day in your life?" If you don't want to work a day in your life, go find a wealthy spouse to fund your lifestyle or something, I don't know. But if you're going to work, don't expect to ever feel like you're not working. Work will always be work, no matter how much you enjoy it. And that's fine. You're allowed to enjoy it, but you're not expected to love it, and it's totally okay if you don't. Liking your career is good enough.

26 Things Average Earners Worry About

THE SERIOUS STUFF

1. Buying a home.

Because *down payments.* According to the National Association of Realtors, the average home price in the United States is expected to be $274,000 in 2020. Just imagine how much higher the average home cost is in pricier areas, like around New York City and San Francisco. How in the actual world can mediocre folk with mediocre salaries afford these prices while also paying for everything else? How?

2. Going to the doctor.

Whenever I go to the doctor, they just send more bills I can't afford to pay, so now I just tell myself "This flu shall pass" whenever I feel sick.

3. The wedding-industrial complex.

Whether you're throwing a wedding for yourself or your adult child, or you're attending one as a guest, weddings have gotten pricey as fuck—and they must be stopped.

4. Procreation.

When you can barely afford to pay for your own lifestyle, how in the world do you suddenly manage to pay for someone else's? Like, do I want children? Yes. But do I also want to keep having the funds available to replenish my wardrobe? Also yes. Help.

5. Family expenses.

Food. Furniture. Clothes. Sports. Braces. Disney World (the happiest and also most expensive place on Earth). A nanny (this is a joke . . . or is it?). Will this money come out of my vagina too?

6. Education.

I feel like you're supposed to start saving for that as soon as you have kids, but if that were the case, I should have started saving to raise babies the minute I came out of the womb.

7. Four-legged family members.

I don't want to have to decide between spending $70 on a cat condo or $70 at the grocery store. I want to be able to buy *both*. And, yes, this is a serious matter.

8. Taking care of aging parents.

No jokes here. This is a serious issue.

9. The final quit.

I find it hard to believe that our average retirement funds will be able to support us in the future, so are we just going to have to work forever or . . . ?

10. Death.

Good cemetery plots and funerals are expensive. Sorry this got morbid, but I'm going to live a fabulous life. I must rest fabulously too. I'm sure all of you feel the same way.

THE EVERYDAY STUFF

11. Paying for discretionary expenditures.

This includes all the things you love to do without going into debt while doing them. For me, this includes Pure Barre, ordering from Sweetgreen, subscribing to Rent the Runway Unlimited, and going to Target (in general). Sure, I pay for these things now, but will I ever be able to *afford* these things? That is the question.

12. Paying back debt and loans.

I feel like these things just keep growing as you age. How do people pay off their debt while it keeps growing? These are life's biggest mysteries.

13. Getting a phone without the upgrade.

Or, let's be realistic—a phone *with* the upgrade. Shit is expensive.

14. Having more than two hair appointments a year.

Okay, maybe this is just me, but hair maintenance for long-haired humans is expensive. The cut, the color, it's a whole thing. I don't care if my split ends and roots are showing. It's simply too expensive for me to go to my nice salon on a regular basis.

15. Having your own Netflix, HBO GO, and Hulu accounts.

Remember to thank your friends' friends' brothers' cousins' ex-fiancé for the login info for now, though.

16. *Going out to dinner and drinks on a regular basis.*

I just want to go to someone's expensive birthday dinner without having a panic attack about owing over $100 for a small amount of food and one drink.

17. *Getting a hotel when visiting friends and family instead of staying in a guest room or, even worse, sleeping on a couch.*

Sure, staying with someone else is free, but it also means you're bound to their schedule and house rules. I like doing what I want when I want, thank you very much.

THE BONUS STUFF

18. *Vacations.*

How are people casually booking trips to different countries multiple times a year? I'm still in debt from a trip I took to the Dominican Republic four years ago. What am I doing wrong here? (see #11)

19. *A nice king-size mattress, like some Tempur-Pedic shit.*

I'm talking five-star-hotel quality. Help me, I need more room to starfish.

20. *Things from Pottery Barn.*

Please close your eyes and imagine yourself walking into Pottery Barn and losing your shit over faux-fur blankets, perfect tablescapes, and woven baskets. Okay, great. Now you understand what it's like to be me.

21. *Hosting holidays.*

Like Thanksgiving. Turkey is fucking expensive. And buying gifts is literally the worst.

22. *A personal trainer.*

All I'm asking for is one-on-one attention on a regular basis. In general, and at the gym. This is how celebrities get in shape. Why does it have to be so pricey for commoners? Huh? Huh?!

23. *Invisalign, veneers, and/or dentures.*

For when our teeth start aging, because you know they will.

24. *A nice designer bag.*

Who are all these people running around with real Louis Vuitton bags? Where are they getting this money? Does it grow on trees? Have I been walking by the wrong trees?

25. *A luxury car.*

To be completely honest, I am perfectly happy with my Honda CR-V, but what if I wanted a luxury car, like an Audi or a Lexus? I'm already struggling to find the funds for literally all of the above, so I'm beginning to think the nice-car thing will never happen for my average self.

26. *Therapy.*

The future sounds very stressful. Let's talk about it.

How I Learned to Embrace Being Unexceptional After Getting Laid Off

"Hey, Samantha, do you have a moment to chat?"

"Of course," I emailed back within seconds. I wondered what the president of my new company wanted to discuss. My phone quickly lit up.

"Hello," I said, after answering.

"Hi, Samantha, it's Robert. So, I'm just going to cut right to the chase. Last night, the investors pulled funding from our budget and have decided to push the company in a different direction. We now have to let several people go, and unfortunately you are one of them." He paused for a few seconds, probably hoping I would give him some sort of response, but I did not say a word. "I know you just started working here the other day, and we tried to tell them that, but they had already made up their minds."

"Okay," I responded. My mind was racing in a thousand different directions. I mean, these people literally just hired me. Budget changing and layoff scheming does not happen overnight. Did they know when they offered me the position that this was coming?

He continued, "Again, we're so sorry this had to happen. We wish you the best of luck."

"Okay," I said before hanging up, unable to get out any other words. But what else was I going to say? I wasn't going to tell him it was okay. It was not okay. I wasn't going to tell him thanks. I was not thankful for anything they had done. I would have said go fuck yourself, but this was the president of a start-up company that just had to lay off 80 percent of its employees. He had already fucked himself.

After I hung up the phone, I sat there, blankly staring at my computer screen for a few seconds before I burst into tears.

It was official. My big, exceptional break was a total bust.

Getting offered a dream job is, well, a dream. You work your ass off for however long it takes to get there, often wondering if you'll *ever* get there or if you're too average to make it big. But then a break comes in the form of a job offer, and it all becomes worth it. Finally, you feel validated. You really are exceptional! Not average at all.

This is what happened to me. After years of trying on jobs like outfits, I was starting to get discouraged. Sure, some jobs fit, but none of them fit perfectly. I always thought I would have this exceptional career. That I had these extraordinary talents that would lead me down an unprecedented path of greatness. But my life was becoming so cut-and-dry. I woke up, went to my regular-person job, went back to my medi- ocre home, went to bed, and woke up the next day to do it all again. Sure, I had big dreams. Much bigger dreams than your standard 9-to-5. But were such dreams actually attain- able for an average person like me?

That's when it happened. Finally, I found the one I had been looking for—and it fit. The role was exactly what I wanted to do. The company did something I actually had an interest in. And the pay was a $20,000 salary increase. It al- most sounded too good to be true, and—spoiler alert that's not really a spoiler alert because you already know—it was.

I had been on such a high celebrating my newly ac- quired job that when I received the news, I couldn't believe it. Just two weeks prior, I had been sitting at my desk at my previous job counting down the minutes until I could leave that mundane role for the new, more exciting one. My ego was already inflated, and it continued to inflate as I humble-bragged about my up-

Why do we find it so hard to be satisfied with jobs that are good enough? Can't we commoners just embrace being unexceptional and celebrate the small accomplishments instead of the Steve Jobs- and Oprah-worthy ones?

coming adventure both in real life and online. That being said, there was a lot of deflating that happened after I got the news, and, like a balloon, the more I deflated, the sadder I became.

I knew being unemployed meant I was going to have to find a new job, stat. But I also knew that finding an exceptional job—a.k.a. one that would meet all of my very high standards—in a short amount of time was going to be a long shot.

I wondered, was I really just meant for an unexceptional career and life? And, if so, what exactly was wrong with that? Why do we find it so hard to be satisfied with jobs that are good enough? Can't we commoners just embrace being unexceptional and celebrate the small accomplishments instead of the Steve Jobs– and Oprah-worthy ones?

This was my first time being laid off. Getting laid off is like being dumped out of nowhere by someone who had literally bankrolled your entire lifestyle and given you access to affordable and decent health insurance. You lose the thing you spent the most time with (isn't it sad that we spend the most waking hours each week at work?), and you don't understand why. You're forced to start anew, but I had personally *just* started anew. I did not want to have to start anew again.

Not to mention, I was embarrassed. No—I was mortified. How was I supposed to face all those people I had humble-bragged to? I couldn't. Was I doomed to stay inside for the rest of my life? No, that would result in my never going to Starbucks again. And I needed my Starbucks.

Speaking of Starbucks—how was I going to afford my venti iced coffees with sugar-free vanilla and almond milk each day as an unemployed member of society? Oh god, was I going to have to sacrifice coffee for the greater good of my bank account?

As one could imagine, financially speaking, I was fucked. But not because I was a reckless money-spending machine. Pretty much anyone who gets laid off is financially fucked. If you have savings, you immediately lose that safety nest egg to important life expenses like rent, mortgages, and debt payments. And if you don't have savings, you better hope you get a severance package, because unemployment benefits don't go very far.

With negative money thanks to debt I had planned to pay off with my new salary and no income, I started to panic. How was I going to pay my bills? How was I going to afford groceries? How was I going to ever pay off my credit cards? How was I *ever* going to save money for the future?

Luckily, I had gotten a termination package, so that was going to be a big help. After I stopped crying, I started to do some basic math. The two months' pay I would be receiving was about equal to four months' pay at my former job due to the salary increase. About five light bulbs turned on in my head.

Sure, I was going to have a hard time finding an exceptional job, but what if I took the next four months to find my own exceptional way of working for myself? I could carefully budget the money I had, figure out all the ways to cut costs, and write. Writing about things I wanted to write about full time for money was my dream, after all, and I figured I was exceptional enough to achieve it. I had read so many success stories about people starting businesses and launching new careers after being laid off. I had thought my former new job was the big break, but maybe, just maybe, being laid off was the real ticket to success.

I called my mom to tell her my idea. And also that I had been laid off.

Her response: "Samantha, you can't do that. What about health insurance? You need a job."

This was valid. Health insurance was important. But why did it always have to get in the fucking way? To get afford- able health insurance, you usually need either a job or a spouse with a job. At this point, my husband, Dan, and I were not married yet. I debated a shotgun wedding, with the baby being my need for health insurance, but I figured it would be insane to rush into marriage for the benefit of health and dental.

I knew my mom was right. After all, I couldn't help my average background. I didn't have a trust fund to pull health insurance money from. I didn't have parents paying my rent. Hell, I didn't even have savings. Dan sure as hell wasn't in a place to fund my lifestyle, and I sure as hell would never let him. I was just an average person trying to get by in an av- erage world. This meant I needed an average job with health insurance.

However, in the meantime, I could try to write on the side while job searching. Part of me knew nothing could realistically come of this, at least not at that point in my life, but part of me was also still hopeful—or more like delusional—that I was exceptional and could somehow become an overnight sensation making millions of dollars all on my own. You never know.

This was my glimmer of hope. And, if you must know, an unemployed person needs a constant glimmer of hope at all times. See, things get tough. Real tough.

Your hopes and dreams get crushed when you lose your job. You try to keep the faith and apply to as many jobs as you're qualified to apply for, but after a while this routine becomes hopeless. The glimmer of hope you're fighting to keep alive begins to fade as the money starts to fade, and you wonder why all of this is happening in the first place.

Did you get laid off because you weren't good enough? Because if you were *really* exceptional, wouldn't you have found a new job by now? Wouldn't someone want you? Are you just not cut out for this world? Should you switch career paths? Should you go back to school for something else?

Negative thoughts like these led to some dark days. I would partially wake up when Dan got out of bed for work at 6 a.m. Before he walked out the door, he would come over to the bed, shake me, and say, "Time to wake up," just like when I was a kid and my mom struggled to get me out of bed for school.

"I'm up," I would respond, rolling over and waiting for him to leave so I could go back to sleep. Why be awake and anxious when I could be asleep and at peace? Sleeping was the obvious right choice for me at this time.

At around 11 a.m., I would roll out of bed and mope from the bathroom to the couch, where I would sit in the dark for hours. Literal hours. I mean, I watched all six seasons of *Gossip Girl* in a week and a half during this time in my life. But what else was I supposed to do? Actually, let me rephrase that: what else could I afford to do?

You know how some people tell you they have no money and can't do something, but then you find out later that they went away for a weekend or attended a concert, and you're like, wait, you told me you didn't have money, but you *definitely* have money—you just didn't want to spend it on *our* plans. You wanted to save it for other plans.

Well, now I legitimately didn't have any money. I guess if you took my debt out of the picture, I had some money, but not enough to "selectively plan" with. Like, if one friend wanted to get dinner and another wanted to go to brunch in one weekend, I couldn't decide which plans I preferred to spend my money on. I couldn't spend my money on either. I had to say no to everything.

I had to use the small amount of money I did have for rent, my car, food, my phone, and other bills. I couldn't gamble on putting that money toward anything else, because if I didn't come up with a way to make a salary again before my money ran out, I wasn't sure what I was going to do.

Not having a job wasn't even the hardest part of being unemployed. It was everything.

It was not being able to spend money, something I had spent my entire life doing without thinking twice.

It was having to say no to plans.

It was spending each and every day alone.

It was the roller coaster of hope and despair that would ascend when I saw a promising job listing and be quickly brought back downhill by silence or a rejection email.

It was sitting on the couch for hours (sometimes days) on end watching Netflix because everything else I could think of doing involved spending money.

It was the struggle of trying to explain my situation to others and realizing a good chunk of the people I interacted with didn't seem to worry about money and/or had never been in a situation where they had to look and interview for jobs before.

It was feeling misunderstood, unappreciated, *embarrassed*, and *average*.

But what was so wrong with being average? Sure, I had big dreams for myself, and sure, I wasn't close to those big dreams at that very moment, but so what? If I were to achieve my dreams so young, what would I have to work for?

The great thing about being average is that you always have something to work toward and look forward to. You're right in the happy medium of life. Financially, you might not be doing amazing, but you have a roof over your head and organic fruits and veggies on the table. You're doing good enough. You might not have the dream job you desire, but you're putting yourself out there and working toward the next step. You're not a deadbeat. So what if success doesn't come overnight—and so what if massive success never comes at all? You're doing fine. You're happy. Since when did that become a crime?

After I finished *Gossip Girl*, I thought about what series I could watch next. Then, I took a good look in the mirror and sighed. What was I doing? This was not me. I was not some exceptional person who had shit handed to her on a silver platter. I was an average person who worked hard for the things she got. But I hadn't been working hard. I had been applying to a few positions a week, hoping and praying one of them would work out so I could stop going to the mandatory career seminars at the unemployment center. I thought of myself as above the situation I was in, when I should have been using it as motivation to get out of it.

Rejection is really just motivation to go after the shit you're meant to have. It wasn't until I came to terms with the fact that I was unexceptional that I realized this. Being unexceptional wasn't a bad thing. It just meant I was normal. Ordinary. And if I wanted to be better than good enough, I'd have to work at becoming extraordinary. I'd have to fight to stand out.

Embracing being unexceptional helped me understand that I can't always get what I want, but damn, I can try. And then I can try again. And again. And again. And I can keep trying until I get (and maybe even truly figure out) exactly what I want. If someone doesn't want me, that's okay. I deserve someone who does. If something doesn't work out, that's fine too. What's meant to actually work out will be better and will lead to greater things.

After accepting this, I started waking up every morning with Dan, even though I had no job to go to. I cleaned our apartment, wrote, cooked, worked out, and, of course, applied to (and sometimes interviewed for) jobs. Every time a rejection came my way, I used it to fuel my job search.

Not long after, I was finally offered a new full-time gig. I felt wanted again. I felt passionate about something. I felt ambitious. I felt happy. Sure, I still felt average, with a mediocre salary and okay title, but all this meant was that I had places to go in this job and out in the world. What mattered most was that I had a job. I was going to be paid to do something I was skilled at again. I realize that sounds as basic as ever, but when it comes down to it, this alone is truly good enough. Not everyone is so lucky.

I was happy my old self was emerging from the dust and rubble, but I could not bring my horrendous spending habits and inflated ego along with her. Losing a steady paycheck was the major kick in the ass I didn't know I needed. Don't get me wrong, getting laid off *sucked*, but damn did it put money in perspective for me. Being unemployed was like a five-month course in "how to not fuck yourself over financially 101." I would honestly not be surprised if this whole ordeal was ordered by my grandmother from the afterworld after she witnessed me buying ten random people a round of shots at a bar. I could imagine her saying, "THIS IS THE

LAST STRAW! I MUST TEACH HER A LESSON!" Being laid off also taught me to be a better person in general.

———

HERE ARE THE most important things I learned when that shit went down:

* *Anything* **can happen at any time to anyone.** You always think things like this could happen, but you never think such things will happen to you. Until they do, of course, and you're left totally fucked, but there's nothing you can do, because, well, you're here and you have to deal with it and get by, prepared or not. Next time, I will be prepared, or at least as much as I can be when it happens, because it will. Average things happen to average people all the time, after all.

* **There is a lot of value in one dollar.** For months, I didn't touch my savings. I lived off of less than half the amount of money I am making now. No, I was not able to save money or pay off debt while I was unemployed, but I learned how to be thrifty and how an average person like me should actually be spending money. I learned the difference between "need" and "want." I learned that I had been throwing a lot of money away on nonsense that I should have been throwing into savings. Now I throw that shit into savings. Thanks, unemployment.

* **You can say no, and people will still love you.** While I was unemployed, I didn't shop. I didn't eat out that much. I stayed in a decent amount, and to my surprise, my friends didn't forget about me. Basically, I lived, but I stopped living as much as I was before, and life still went on.

* **Small accomplishments are accomplishments, too.** I never used to let myself celebrate the little things, because they weren't exceptional. I was so laser-focused on making others see me as special and talented that I lost sight of what I was accomplishing on my journey to the bigger accomplishments. Never lose sight of those things. They are arguably more important than celebrating the end goal, because they're the things that are going to get you there!

* **Nothing will be handed to you without sacrifice, hard work, and rejection, so get OK with that.** Life is tough, and shit happens. If you think you're above that, I'm sorry, but I cannot pity you for pitying yourself. No one is above rejection. No one is above making mistakes. This is how we learn and grow. If you're not learning or growing, you're not doing it right. No one finds success by sitting on their ass, except the Kardashians, but we can't all have Kris Jenner as a mom-ager so . . .

The Financial Burn Book

A LIST OF EXPENSES THAT EXCEED
OUR JUST-OKAY INCOMES

Your Rent or Mortgage
"Causes super jumbo debt"

Always approximately half of your monthly pay, no matter how much you make. Always above and beyond what your home feels like it's worth. For me, my rent is always increasing for literally no reason. It's not like my home is getting bigger and better. It stays the same and somehow becomes more expensive. Does this make sense? No. Someone cancel my rent. I'm just kidding—I need a place to live. Guess I'll keep throwing my paycheck at my rent instead of saving to buy a house so I can pay a mortgage instead. What a twisted cycle we average people live in, right?

Birthday Dinners
"Too self-involved to function"

Always somewhere that has salads for over $15. Always awkward when the bill comes. Always includes at least one person you don't like (maybe two). Always at an inconvenient time, solely because there is no such thing as a convenient time for someone else's birthday dinner. Never *really* wanted by the person whose birthday it is. But after succumbing to and paying for other peoples' birthday dinners, you have to plan your own. It's only fair.

Vacations
"Made out with FOMO"

Always beyond what you can actually afford. Always stressful before, during, and after, even though they're supposed to cause 24/7 relaxation. Never the way your Instagram photos make it look. Never exactly what you were hoping. Never long enough. Never often enough. Never fully paid off. Always necessary though.

Cars
"An overpriced little byotch"

Always taking money out of your bank account every month. Always needing additional money from your bank account for maintenance. Occasionally needing even *more* money from your bank account so as to not die. Eventually going to die, but you can just get a new one when that happens. Which brings me to my next point: why are we so quick to shut cars out of our lives and get new ones when we are taught not to treat people like that? If cars are so disposable, shouldn't they cost less money? Like how disposable cameras cost less than real ones? I mean, what is this shit?

Alcohol
"Has an amazing ability to suppress reality"

Always there, no matter what. Always able to laugh with you again after a fight or rough patch, like nothing happened. Basically family.

A New Outfit
"Fabulous, but evil"

Never necessary. Never a perfect fit, but you rushed to buy it because, well, you wanted a new outfit. Never noticed by anyone except you. In fact, no one would have noticed if you'd worn a repeat outfit instead—yes, even if it had been photographed and posted online. Never worn more than once. Always a waste of money.

Fitness Classes
"Gives you a nice ass"

Always overpriced. Always making you feel like you need nicer workout clothes, leading you to buy new workout clothes. Always fun to talk about going to. Never fun to actually go to, unless you have new workout clothes to show off. [Almost] always worth it.

Gifts
"Too nice to function"

Why should you go broke because someone else chose to do a thing? You had no part in this thing. You are not doing the thing. You are just an innocent bystander in a series of shower invites and charity donation requests. SOS.

Any Event Where You're Hosting Friends
"I am a fun pusher. A SAD OLD FUN PUSHER."

Always stressful. Always the cause of a lot of anxiety. Always too overwhelming to really enjoy. Always involving unnecessary purchases you didn't need to make in order to please people. Never cancelable. A great excuse to clean your home, though, if the party is at your place.

THE

I DO SHIT I ENJOY!

AWARD

2

IN PRAISE OF SUBPAR SOCIAL LIVES

. . . and other thoughts about fair-weather friendships and sporadic get-togethers

How to Make New Friends
When You Have Suboptimal Social Skills

"Hey!" I texted her while sitting on the subway headed to the restaurant. "Looking forward to tonight. What are you wearing, just so I know how to find you?"

"Hi, Sam! Me too. I'll be in a gray sweater and jeans. See you soon!" she texted back.

I looked down at my outfit. Black leather leggings, a taupe-colored silky blouse, black booties. My eyes grew wide, and my throat became dry. What was I thinking when I put this shit on? I was far too overdressed for the occasion. What was she going to think of me? Why had I even agreed to this? What kind of idiot says yes when asked to go to dinner with someone they met on Twitter?

Her name was Lianne, and we followed each other on the social media network.

We had never met in real life, but we both worked in the media industry and clearly shared the same love of witty online banter. After a few months of liking each other's tweets, Lianne messaged me asking for my email. A few minutes later, I had a message in my inbox. She said she was new to the area and asked if I would ever want to get a drink with her. I responded yes, and we figured out the details.

While I was thrilled about having a new contact in the media industry, I was also excited about making a potential new friend. Sure, I had a decent number of friends already, but I was always open to more. I just had literally no idea where or how to find them. I mean, seriously, how in the world was I supposed to make new friends when I had mediocre social skills and an unexceptional social life? Was it even possible? Was I just doomed to forever chase after old fleeting friendships?

The friends I currently had were all so different than me. We worked in different fields, lived in different places, preferred different social scenes, and were beginning to gravitate toward different lifestyles. I worried about what I would do if all those friendships faded. Even if they all did stick around, part of me wished I had at least one friend who was more like me. Could Lianne be that person? She worked in media. She enjoyed spamming her followers on Twitter. *This could be a match*, I thought.

I had never done this before—the "friend date" thing. Was this even a friend date? I wasn't sure. Did Lianne just want to network? I felt like a teenage girl, unsure if the guy she was meeting at the movie theater on Friday night had asked her to hang out as a friend or as something more than that. Clearly, my outfit said I was expecting something different than she was. But what was she expecting, exactly?

After getting off the T, I walked around the corner to the restaurant. As I approached the front doors and saw how crowded it was inside, I panicked. I hated going places alone where I would be forced to use my mediocre social prowess. Every summer during my youth, I would find a friend to attend overnight camp with me because I was afraid if I went alone, my personality would retreat into my shell of a body and not come out of hiding until I was around people I knew again. I would also bring stashes of candy for the sole purpose of bribing people to be my friend. I wished I had a friend—or a stash of candy—with me at that moment to help break the ice.

Once inside the restaurant, I looked around for the girl in the gray sweater sitting alone at a table for two. Then I spotted her. Hair up, glasses on, à la Kitty Sanchez from *Arrested Development*, except way cooler. Was she even wearing makeup? I couldn't tell, even as I got closer to the table.

I did notice she was wearing sneakers, though, which for some reason escalated my anxiety. I had tried so hard to look impressive for this dinner that I had put on my boots with fucking *heels*.

"Lianne?" I asked.

She put down the menu and smiled. "Sam! Hi! It's so great to finally meet you!" She hopped off her stool to stand up and leaned in for the hug. I hugged back.

I took off my jacket and placed it on the back of my chair. "You too! Sorry I'm so overdressed. Coming from work. You know how it is," I lied. I had gone home and changed after work. I had also woken up an hour earlier than usual that day to curl my hair for this occasion, but that is neither here nor there.

For the next hour, we chatted over wine and cheese. Eventually, the check came. As I was signing the check, Lianne stood up and started putting on her jacket. "Thanks for meeting me tonight. This was fun!"

"It was!" I said, debating if I should say we should do it again. What if she didn't want to hang out again? What if she didn't like me? What if she didn't like me because I talked about work too much? What if she didn't like me because I didn't talk about work enough? I felt like I was far too unimpressive during this friend date to bring up the possibility of a second one.

We gave each other a quick ass-out hug, said our goodbyes, and left the restaurant. I realized we were about to encounter the awkwardness that is walking to the same place (the T station), so I went in the opposite direction, figuring I could take a little detour. On my detour, I sent a group text to the friends I already had: "What's everyone up to this weekend? Anyone want to hang out?"

Why was it so easy for me to retreat back to the familiar, but so scary to explore the unknown? The friends I already had were the familiar. Even if they did shut me down when I brought up prospective plans, I at least knew they did in fact like me as a human, despite all my flaws. New friends, though, were unknown. I didn't know how they'd react to my flaws. I didn't know if they would find my unexceptional life interesting. I didn't know if they would think I was good enough to hang out with again.

After our friend date, Lianne and I never talked again. Years later, I'm not sure if she felt the same way as me and was too nervous to reach out after, or if she was simply not impressed by my mediocrity and was glad I never followed up with her. To be honest, I'm not even sure she still knows who I am. I know who she is though. And not because I still follow her on Twitter. Because she was my first and only friend date in my thirty years on this earth, and I will never forget that.

That's right. Since our failed friend date, my subpar social skills have made me far too nervous to put myself out there on the new-friend market. But at the same time, my life has been zooming by, and a

> My subpar social skills made me too nervous to put myself out there on the new-friend market.

number of my friendships have faded. This has only fed my appetite for new friends—and let me tell you, I am starving. But my unexceptional lifestyle is totally getting in the way.

Life for average people is basically just a cycle of waking up, going to work, taking care of yourself and your family, going to bed, and repeating, while maybe forcing yourself to occasionally fit in things like getting a morning coffee without being more than fifteen minutes late to work and making the trek to the gym when all you want to do is cover your couch in Elmer's glue and lie down. So, how and when are average people supposed to find time to make new friends (never mind manage to keep the old ones around too)? There are no set times or designated places to make new friends, which often doesn't bother you because, well, you already have friends (and a lack of time to spend with them). But, over time, as more friends fade and you start losing touch with more people, you will realize that having a few new friends couldn't hurt.

So, what do you do? How do average people make new friends?

How Average People Can Make Good-Enough Friendships at Work

Work is not equal to school. Not everyone is in the same situation as you are, and no one is there to make friends. There is no bell that rings for lunch, calling everyone to congregate in the kitchen to socialize at the same time. There is no gymnastics team, nor is there a cheerleading team to be your last resort (that was a *Bring It On* joke, people). There are no extracurricular activities at all. Socializing about life on a surface level (i.e., the weather, the vaguest description of what you're doing this weekend) is mandatory, but socializing to form real bonds with other humans? That shit is optional.

Over the years, I've made some friends at work, but it has never been the same as making friends at school. Each time I thought I had made a real, legitimate friend at work, as soon as one of us went off to a new job, they vanished. A piece of them was left on my social media feeds, but the communication between us died (oh, the irony of social media, I know).

So, can work ever actually be an option for making new friends, or will the friendships always fade as soon as you don't have the same boss to complain about anymore?

I sometimes feel like I was supposed to make work friends when I was younger—like I missed my window to form new friendships at work. I rarely have time to socialize after hours on weeknights, and, if I do, I usually have plans with an old friend whom I never get to see. On the weekends, I'm almost always booked, leaving minimal to no time for hanging out with work friends. That's probably why I can never keep work friends after we are no longer co-workers, and that's probably why they have trouble staying in touch with me. There are only so many people you can make time for outside of your typical 9-to-5 job.

Then there's the whole issue of whether making friends in the workplace is a good idea to begin with. Over the years, I've learned you should keep work separate from your personal life. You don't want to vent about coworkers to someone you can't trust, and friendships are built on trust. You need to see if you can trust someone before becoming true friends, but is risking your career to test those waters worth it? I don't think so. That's why I live my work life by this motto: "Like everyone. Trust no one."

The best thing an average soul can do when it comes to making new friends in the workplace is to focus on making good-enough connections to help you get through the day. And if one day one of those good-enough connections remains after you are no longer on the same payroll, you will know you made a *real* new friend, and the unexceptional effort you put into your mediocre work-lationships will all be worth it.

How Unimpressive People Can Find Friends Through a Shared Activity

The only place I regularly frequent that isn't my apartment or work (or Starbucks) is my barre studio, Pure Barre. Since I started taking barre classes five years ago, I've become friendly with approximately three people. This does not include the teachers. The teachers and I are friendly, but I'm pretty sure that's only because they are paid to be friendly to clients. We can ignore this fact, because I like believing they are my in-real-life friends. It helps me drag my lazy ass to class when I don't want to go.

Barre class, in a way, reminds me of the dance classes I took growing up. I have to be there at a certain time. There are mirrors everywhere in which I can judge myself. It's for sure overpriced. There are moves involved that we used to do during ballet. However, it is also very different. For starters, it's a fifty-minute workout class. I can decide when I want to go and when I don't want to go. There are choreographed routines involved, but none we have to learn and perform at a recital. The biggest difference: it's not a team atmosphere. Because I was on a dance team growing up, I took classes with the same people multiple days a week for years. We got to know each other, and some friendships were made.

When I first started taking barre, I thought maybe, just maybe, I would make a new friend or two at the studio. I mean, why not? All of us taking the classes had one huge thing in common: we all raced home from work to impose an immense amount of pain on our bodies through fifty minutes of pure hell (this was an unintentional Pure Barre joke)—and we all loved it. So much so that we wore tank tops and sweatshirts branded with the barre studio's logo. It was a cult, and people in a cult are usually close. So, why haven't I really gotten to know any of the people in my cult?

There is this one group of women who attend the same classes as me who are all friends. I often think about how they got to know one another, and if one day I could ever break into their clique. Like, did they meet during class?

Or did they know each other from outside of class? During class, how do they find time to talk? My unexceptional self is always barging into the studio at the last second, taking the last spot available, and after class I grab my stuff and run to the Trader Joe's next door to buy more frozen meals I don't need. Am I supposed to be getting to class early and sticking around after, hoping someone will talk to me?

There have been days when I've gotten to class at a reasonable time and struck up conversation with familiar faces around me. I've even connected with a few of those people on social media and have done the whole "let's get drinks some time" with each of them. But it has never gone past that. No one has set a date and time for this to happen. Could I be the one to initiate this? Sure. But not only am I always either busy or tired, but my so-so social skills also freeze in the face of potential rejection.

What we commoners need to do while attending events and participating in activities with others who share a common interest with us is stop worrying about not being good enough to fit in. We are all out there struggling together, some showing it more than others—during a workout, a networking event, a class, and throughout life in general. Never assume you are below average compared to others, because, chances are, people probably feel the same way as you do about a lot of things, no matter how they appear. So, take a chance. Get to know people. Talk to the person you're always bumping into at the gym. Ask the person you sit next to in the class you're taking to grab a coffee with you. Tell the person you had a great conversation with at a networking event that you should get together some time—and actually follow up. Make real plans. Go from there. You will never know until you try, and when it's not the workplace, you've really got nothing to lose.

How to Make New Friends Who Aren't Involved in Your Everyday Happenings

If I am not at work or barre class, you can probably find me on the couch, finishing a television series I just started (one cannot simply watch just one episode anymore) while scrolling through Instagram, on the phone complaining to my mom about something, at Target buying glass llamas and throw pillows, or hanging out with the friends I already have. As you can see, I don't exactly put myself in many situations where it's easy to make new friends.

All of the (very few) new friends I've made as an adult were introduced to me through mutual friends. I can't rely on this method of making new friends, though, because it happens quite rarely. When I spend time with friends now, I prefer to do so in a setting where I can have meaningful catch-up sessions with them and discuss our lives. That's not easy to do when a third party is brought into the mix.

So, if I want to use my friends to make new friends, am I supposed to have them set me up on blind friend dates? I mean, I've actually had friends tell me that I would love their coworker and that I would get along so well with one of their friends I've never met. Am I supposed to respond to these claims by asking my friends to "set me up"? Or maybe I could suggest a double friend date. Maybe I have a friend who would get along with my friend, too.

I've never embraced such situations, because they always scream "awkward" to me. Why? When someone unfamiliar is brought into a familiar group of people, the vibe becomes higher than surface level. In those situations, you have to actively partake in conversations that take effort and work and *try* to get to know someone. The problem? Trying is the worst. No one likes trying.

But if you want new friends, you have to be willing to try. I mean, friendships are really just marriage without the fancy wedding, commitment to one person, and legal bullshit. You have to put yourself out there, get to know people, and work to maintain connections if you want to form a friendship and then make it last.

I know plenty of people who have joined adult sports teams and gone to meet-ups for people with similar interests with the hope of finding a romantic fling. Instead, they ended up walking away with new friends. I mean, this is pretty much the plot of *The Bachelor* franchise. The series is not just a quest for Instagram followers. It is also a quest for friendships. And love too, sometimes, but that is debatable.

So, how can we average people branch out of our own ordinaries to make new friends? Well, we can add extra ordinaries to our life itineraries! We can do something crazy like move to a new city, surrounding ourselves with new places, things, and people. Or we can stick to what we know and find people who know a thing or two about those things too. We can find groups for average people anywhere, full of humans who do things like own dogs, run marathons, and work in certain industries. Basically, we just need to try, and we can start by putting our average selves out there into the average world.

The Most Important Thing Average People Need to Know Before Setting Out to Make Those New Friends

When it comes down to it, all an ordinary person like you really needs to do to make new friends is shake off your lack of confidence and use it to find friendships instead. You don't need to be impressive to make new friends. In fact, that could turn people off from wanting to bring you into their life. Knowing you're flawed, just like everyone else, makes you an ideal person to bond with, laugh with, and grow with. Being ordinary means you're just like everyone else. You're relatable. Embrace it. Own it.

Knowing you're flawed, just like everyone else, makes you an ideal person to bond with, laugh with, and grow with. Being ordinary means you're just like everyone else. You're relatable. Embrace it. Own it.

Sometimes I wonder what my friend date with Lianne would have been like if I had embraced being unimpressive rather than focusing so hard on trying to impress her. Would we have found more in common? Would she have asked me to hang out again? Would the two of us be backpacking across Europe right now? Would she have chosen me to be in her wedding? Would she have introduced me to her kids? By embracing my own flaws, I could have changed my life by acquiring a new friend. Now, I'll never know . . . but I'll *always* wonder.

When Your Ordinaries Become Opposite, Can You Still Be Friends?

One of my biggest fears is that as time goes on, I will keep losing friends. Like what if one day I wake up and they are all gone? What if one day I am a mother of a bunch of teen- agers who are never around, with a husband who is always working, and I suddenly realize I spent the past twenty years forgetting to respond to friends' text messages and am now alone? Is that where my life is headed (minus the husband- too-busy-for-his-wife thing—no husband of mine will ever be too busy for me)? Most of the adults in my life are living similar lifestyles. As an average, unexceptional soul, am I doomed for this no matter what?

I always knew that losing friends over time was normal. I just never thought it would happen to me. I thought my friendships were stronger than the marriages of Barack and Michelle, Tom Hanks and Rita Wilson, and SJP and Ferris Bueller all combined. What I found is they were more like the relationships of Pete and Ariana, Jen and Ben, and Kim and Kris Humphries. Fun for a while, but not meant to last forever.

As I've watched some of my own friendships fade, I've realized that many of them were not actually friendships.

I was so focused on proving how impressive I was by having an abnormally large number of acquaintances that I lost sight of the importance of connecting with people on more than just a surface level. Surface friendships were what I had a lot of. Meaningful friendships were what I was lacking.

That wasn't the only reason I started losing friends in my twenties. Things were changing. People were moving in new directions, literally and figuratively. They were becoming busy with their own lives. Hell, I was becoming busy with my own life. Our lifestyles were just not syncing up, and our ordinaries were becoming opposite.

I began to wonder if friendships were based on being the same type of mediocre. So, if your everyday lifestyles involve completely different things, like living in the suburbs with your spouse and kids versus living the single life in the city (potentially with a roommate—life is expensive, no matter your age), can you still be friends? If your idea of fun involves a night on the couch in yoga pants sans bra and makeup watching television, but their idea of fun involves getting dressed to the nines to go out on the town, can you still be friends? If your idea of a lot of money is their idea of a small amount, when it comes to doing anything together that involves spending money (which is just about 90 percent of all social-based activities, if I'm being honest here), can you still be friends?

Spoiler alert: You can.

Let me tell you a story.

How to Be Friends with People Who Don't Share the Same Everyday Life as You

I was at the nail salon, sitting in a massage chair and scrolling through my emails, when my phone started ringing.

"Are you going to answer that?" my friend, Zoe, who was sitting next to me, asked.

I stared at the phone for another second, confused. "It's Rachel; she wants to Facetime." Rachel and I barely talked on the phone with each other anymore, let alone videochatted. I knew what was happening. "I have to, she probably got engaged."

I swiped to answer, and instead of being met by Rachel's face, I was met by a shiny diamond waving around on a dirty, cracked iPhone screen. I let out the staged scream that is encouraged but not required by females getting married everywhere. "You're engaged!" I yelled as quietly as possible to avoid embarrassing myself at the packed salon.

Suddenly, the screen switched to Rachel's overjoyed face before panning over to her fiancé and then back to her.

"Congratulations, you guys! This is so exciting! I'm so happy for you!" Did I have to give more praise? I wasn't sure. I had never done this before. Rachel was officially my first friend to get engaged.

I let out another shriek of excitement to buy myself time while coming up with my next move. I had learned from many a rom-com that the next logical question for me to ask was "How did he pop the question?" but my vocal cords froze at the thought. There were two reasons for this. 1.) No one should ever "pop" the question out of nowhere. This is a fucking lifelong commitment. You can't just spontaneously decide to propose marriage one day without having ever discussed it. 2.) Who was I to assume HE asked the question? Does the guy always really ask the question in all heterosexual relationships? And if so, why? Women are capable of asking this question, too.

"How did this happen?!" I decided to go with. However, to be completely honest, I really didn't care. I just wanted to know more details about her ring. But I refrained from asking. After all, it was more important to celebrate my newly engaged friend for deciding to partner in life with someone, bound by taxes and 401ks until she was old and wrinkly with boobs sagging south of her vagina, than the fact that she had gotten an expensive piece of jewelry that she would get to parade around until death (or divorce) did them part.

As soon as our conversation ended and I hung up the phone, Zoe looked at me and said, "Your friendship with Rachel is totally about to change."

I didn't understand, though. Rachel and I had been friends for years. Why would things change between us just because she was getting married, while I was nowhere close to it?

Over the next year, Rachel filled my text-message inbox with the trials and tribulations of wedding planning, which I did not understand. Watching her partake in the wedding-planning frenzy made me wonder how the fuck one gets to a point in one's life where one cares more about flower arrangements and DIY projects than literally anything else. Was every bride like this? I wondered if, when I became a bride one day, I would stop thinking all wedding dresses looked the same and grow an affinity for centerpieces.

A few years later, I was planning a wedding myself. Finally, I thought, I had caught up to Rachel. I could recite the name of every flower in the book, and I had visited the wedding aisle at Michael's so many times that I could navigate it with a blindfold on. I tried reaching out to Rachel to discuss my newfound interests with her, but she had no interest. Time had passed. She had moved on. We had different lives.

Did this mean our friendship was fated to fade? Did she find my interests and life events unimportant compared to her own because she was now a mom? Did she find my accomplishments unimpressive compared to her own feat of purchasing a home? Did she find me suboptimal to spend time with because my lifestyle was too below-average compared to her own?

When Rachel and I first met, we bonded over shared interests. At the time, I figured that because we were so similar, we would always be close, but I was now starting to think that our shared interests were not enough. Perhaps shared interests were only there to spark an attraction between two people, and a similar lifestyle was the glue needed to keep those people together.

As I watched our friendship change, I became paranoid about my other friendships.

Were my single friends going to eventually disappear because I was married? If I moved to the suburbs, would my friends living in the city vanish? If I had a kid, would my friends without kids disappear? If my everyday became different from their everyday, would they eventually dissolve from the picture?

When we first became friends, we were all so goddamn similar. All of us. How did things change so quickly? How did a bunch of people who are the same age, who come from similar backgrounds, who'd once had the same daily schedules and weekend night plans suddenly start living such different lives?

Sometimes I wonder whether if I met my friends today, we would still be friends. If I met Rachel today at work, would we ever make plans to get drinks or coffee, or would we find nothing in common with each other and act as acquaintances? I mean, had I known whose lives would turn out similar to mine, would I now have a completely different friend group?

The answer: I hope not.

Have you ever seen a show on television where the friends are all just like one another? No, right? They are *always* stereotypes. You have the single one, the married one, the divorced one, the rich one, the struggling one, the party animal, the parent. If all the friends were the same, it would make for pretty fucking boring television. It would also make for a pretty fucking boring reality. How can life stay interesting if everything around you is the same?

Having shared interests or being in similar situations may help one *make* a friendship, but these things certainly do not keep a friendship. You are responsible for that. So how can you go about this? Let's discuss.

On Finding the Happy Medium of Making Time for People You Care About

Maintaining a friendship is hard work. Not only does it take all that effort, but it also takes time. And what average person has a bunch of time to prolong a bunch of friendships? None.

So, what is an average person to do when it comes to being a good-enough friend and keeping in touch with people? Well, for starters, call your fucking friends. This is a very hypocritical thing for me to say because I have a fear of using my phone to talk to people with my actual voice. I have been this way since I was a kid. My mom used to hand me the phone when I was in grade school, encouraging me to call so-and-so for a playdate, and I would just stare at her, terrified to reach out to any and all classmates, because what if they didn't want anything to do with my subpar self?

Today, nothing has changed. Sometimes I can hear my mom telling me, "You can't just expect people to always come to you, Samantha! You have to be the one to reach out, too," just like she did when I was younger. But the thought of calling an acquaintance or a friend who possibly does not want to talk to me at that moment is an anxiety attack waiting to happen. Add in the thought of calling that someone *without a reason, just to talk*, and you will find me on the floor, RIP.

Thank god for texting. But that can be problematic too.

While being able to be in constant communication with people is a blessing, it is also a curse. Because of technology, we assume we're supposed to be in touch with people all the time, and that if we don't respond in a quick-enough manner, we are doing a poor job at communicating. But there was once a time when you couldn't be in touch with people this much, and guess what? Friendships still existed. That means they can still exist today even if you're not exceptional at talking to people you care about all the time. It also means it's okay if you're not good at talking to people all the time.

To make time for the people you care about, you need to find the happy medium when it comes to staying in touch. This means you don't have to reach out to people constantly, but you should check in every once in a while. You don't have to see each other a lot, but you should make plans to see each other every now and then. You don't have to answer texts right away, but you should try to answer them eventually.

All you really have to do is make time for people. After all, being busy is a hoax. I know you have some wiggle room in your planner for the next month. And also at least some time allotted to relax. Spend it wisely.

Why Being a Good-Enough Friend Is Good Enough

I often wonder if my friends feel like they're below average at maintaining friendships, too. Maybe they also fear the phone, and maybe they too suck at texting. Or maybe everyone except me talks on the phone to people all the time and texts back and forth with people all day every day, despite their demanding workloads and busy schedules. Maybe I am the shittiest of the shittiest. The lowest of the low. The girl who thought she had all the friends in the world but who later found out that while she was busy thinking about her friendships, everyone else was busy having deep, meaningful conversations with each other about life.

This is so far from the truth, though. In reality, everyone is out there trying to balance their friendships and their lives. If being average were a job, the job description would be, like, sixty-eight pages long. It's impossible to be great at everything when you're doing a million little things. But no one is really expecting you to be great, except you (and maybe your parents, but they need to calm the fuck down if so), so you need to be satisfied with doing good enough.

Good enough is often the best you can do with what's handed to you, so if you're being a good-enough friend, power to you. You're doing awesome.

11 Less-Than-Average Friends It's Okay to Lose

1. *The friend who is always busy*

Me: "Hey! What are you up to this weekend?"
Friend: "Staying in tonight, family party on Saturday."
Me: "Oh cool, we need to hang out soon!"
Friend: "Yes, definitely."

Me: "Hey! Are you around this weekend so we can actually hang?"
Friend: "Ahh, I'm not. I'm out of town until Monday."
Me: "Of course! Well, let's plan something soon. It's been too long."
Friend: "For sure."

Me: "Hey! Would you want to get dinner one night this week?"
Friend: "Work is insane, sorry, maybe another week."
Me: "Yeah, work sucks. Okay!"

PEOPLE. THIS IS when you throw in the towel. You have no idea how many times I've had variations of this text conversation with people I thought were friends. Perhaps they were actually busy all the times I reached out, but if they really cared, they would have followed up and suggested a time to get together that worked for them. Most of them didn't though. At first, this upset me because it fucking sucks when friendships fade, but then I was like wait—*everyone* is busy, but no one has a filled calendar 24/7. If these people were average friends, they would make an effort to see me. But our friendships were not average. They were no longer friendships at all. Which, honestly, good. The fewer people I have to put effort into seeing in my own busy schedule, the better. There's perks to everything, people. Moral of the story: if someone doesn't give a shit about you, stop giving a shit about them.

2. The toxic friend

Whether they judged you for your own actions, or you judged them for theirs, your differing opinions on what is average do not make for a healthy friendship. Maybe they think you go out too much. Maybe you think they're immature. Maybe they think you're boring because you don't socialize with people enough. Maybe you don't like their partner. Maybe they don't think you're living up to your full potential. Maybe you think they're living beyond their means.

Whatever the case, friendships *can* survive these things. But if someone cannot accept you for the average human being you are, do you want to be their friend? No, thank you. And if you cannot accept someone for who they are, do you want them making you anxious forever? No, thank you, again. Something that is toxic is not meant to remain by your side forever. It's waste, so trash it.

3. The friend who moved across the country and then you mostly lost touch

I used to say that couples who rushed to move in together were smart because they would figure out pretty quickly if they were wasting each other's time. I like to think friends who move across the country from one another go through a similar test. You can easily find out if your friendship is real or if you were just "friends by proximity"—a.k.a. friends who are close based on being physically close to one another. Over the years, I learned I had a handful of "friends by proximity" when we lost touch after our zip codes lost similarities. There was nothing to talk on the phone about anymore and no reason for texts. The good thing about this "friendship test" is that you'll discover which friendships are legitimate. For example, one of my best friends lives in Los Angeles, and I talk to her more than I do some friends who live two miles away in Boston. That's when you know.

4. The friend who lives more than two miles away whom you never see

It's all about that initial decision to leave your couch—when it's worth it, it's worth it, no matter how far the drive is. Over the years, I've realized that I am not "worth it" for some people, and that some people are not "worth it" for me. See, I love being home. I love watching TV. I love my couch. I love sleeping. There's limited time in my weeks for me to do the things I love, so you have to be really fucking worth it for me to get up from the depths of the down throw pillows on my couch. That being said, I totally understand and accept if I'm not worth it for other people. I have things to do (and not do?) anyway; bye.

5. The friend you were always texting first, and when you stopped texting so did they

Picture me constantly reaching out to someone, asking things like, "What's up?"; "How is everything going?!"; "How is work?"; and "What are you doing this weekend?" Picture that person never doing the same. Over time, this type of shit leads to anxiety taking over my body, because why do I keep reaching out to someone who never reaches out to me? There have been a few instances where I just stopped texting such people and left the ball in their court. Most of those people never reached out. That's because one-sided friendships are not friendships. It's as simple as that. It's not like I don't have enough friends who actually reach out to me, anyway.

6. The old coworker

No one goes to work to make friends, but because you're with these people almost every day of the week for approximately eight hours each day, you at least become acquainted with your coworkers. Sometimes you even become actual friends. Maybe you get drinks together occasionally when you leave the office to complain about work. Maybe you hang out with each other's friends and families over the weekend. But whether you were acquaintances or legitimate friends, when one of you leaves for a new job, the friendship *rarely* continues. People you once talked to every day just vanish.

To the 1 percent of work friendships that last beyond working together, I applaud you. I would say tell me your secrets, but I already have trouble maintaining my current friendships. Adding former coworkers would be impossible.

7. The friend who got a new significant other

Whenever I've been in a relationship, I've always made sure to spend an equal amount of time with my significant other and my friends. Not everyone is like this, though. Some people just really fucking suck at multitasking. They go all-in on time with their significant other, rarely making an effort to see their friends. I've seen people do this and then have trouble getting back in touch with friends after break-ups. It's not healthy.

Something else I've seen: the friend who becomes a completely different person after entering a relationship— potentially a person you do not care to be friends with. Maybe their significant other is now always with them when you hang out, or maybe their personality has changed. But whether or not you like the person they have become, your friendship is different. All because they started dating someone new. When this happens, you have to ask yourself: is this person showing their true colors? Were they like this all along? Then, you have to decide to either go with it or move on. You can't control someone else's love life.

8. The friend who is fun but not good

His name was Derek. My group of friends welcomed him with open arms because the more, the merrier. Derek was fun. Derek was nice. Derek was always down to hang out. Over time though, Derek became an asshole—actually, no, we just realized he had been an asshole the whole time.

Everyone knows a Derek. He's the mooch. The meddler. The manipulator. The instigator. The one whose commentary makes you second-guess your association. Derek was fun, but there's a difference between someone who is fun and someone who is a friend. Maybe you haven't realized you have a Derek in your life yet, but maybe this will help you realize you do.

9. The friend your mom was right about

Growing up, my mom would always tell me when she didn't like one of my friends. "I just get a vibe," she would say about the friend when I asked for her reasoning. I didn't understand. I loved all of my friends and thought of myself as an excellent judge of character.

I always wondered what she meant by this, until I eventually started to get the vibe from these people, too. My mom claimed some people were too self-involved and stuck up, and she said others were bad influences. It took me a while to realize it, but she was right, and as time went on, these friendships faded. These people ended up going down paths that I chose not to follow. The paths my mom predicted they would each end up going down.

Moral of this story: moms are usually right when it comes to your friendships. Never doubt that mom vibe.

10. *The friend you've had the same plans to grab a drink with for five years*

Once upon a time, you were close with this person. But then you moved to different places, ran in different circles, or had a falling out you'd since thought about repairing. Long story short: you stopped talking. Now, every time you run into this friend or reach out to them about something, it always ends with the following conversation:

You: "We have to get together soon."
Them: "Yes, it's been WAY too long."
You: "When are you free?"
Them: "Well, I'm busy the next couple of weekends, but what about next month?"

You: "Maybe. I just have to check my calendar."
Them: "Yes! Let's check our calendars and pick a date."
You: "Absolutely!"
Them: "Great!"

BUT YOU NEVER follow up and pick a date, and neither do they. And then a few months or two years later, you find yourselves connecting for some reason and have the same exact conversation. Basically, STOP TRYING TO MAKE DRINKS HAPPEN WITH EACH OTHER; IT'S NOT GOING TO HAPPEN. And that is okay. It's perfectly normal to text an acquaintance occasionally without worrying about making plans to see each other. You don't have to become friends with these people again.

11. The friend who got too wrapped up in his or her own world to have time for yours

It's not that this friend is too busy for you. They have invited you many times to come see the dog, house, baby, etc. and to events they are planning. But when it comes to one-on-one time with you, they're never up for it. When it comes to events you're planning, they're never around.

Sure, you guys might text on a regular basis, but friend-ship is more than just a text every now and then. You have to make time for each other's worlds, not just for each other. This friend is definitely the hardest to accept losing. It's not that anything went wrong, or that one of you doesn't like the other. You are just living two different, ordinary lives, and they aren't meshing together anymore.

How to Have a Social Life That's Good . . . Enough

There is an episode of *Sex and the City* where Carrie is in bed for the night and gets a phone call from an acquaintance, who invites her out to a bar. This prompts her to get out of bed, put on a full face of makeup, do her hair, put on an outfit complete with heels, and head out the door to meet a friend.

What?

Why?

Who would do this? A psycho? Yes, only a psycho.

While obviously this is a television show, and Carrie Bradshaw is a fictional person, I once longed to have a social life as exciting and extraordinary as hers. Turns out, though, my social life was quite extra ordinary compared to hers.

Monday through Friday, at age 27, I would go to my regular-person 9-to-5 job, just like everyone else. Then, maybe, if I was feeling ambitious, I'd work out. And at the end of the day, I would go home, take off my bra, and eat cheese for dinner while watching *SVU* marathons on the couch. I'm totally kidding. I didn't partake in this scenario that often. (Or did I?)

My weekends were always jam-packed with errands, family things, events usually celebrating other people, and mediocre plans with friends—at least compared to what we considered "exciting" years ago. If I did somehow have a plan-free weekend, I'd go off the grid, exhausted from life thus far, praying that no one contacted me, so I could spend my weekend in peace. Peace meaning me on the couch sans bra, with pizza, and also maybe taking a trip to Target.

Was my social life really meant to be this dull? As a self-proclaimed extrovert, I have always been an extremely sociable person. I love being around people. I always thought that because of this, I'd have a marvelous social calendar. But that was not the case. My social life was subpar. It was basic and ordinary. It was the exact opposite of what I thought it would be.

If we're going to lean even more into this *Sex and the City* thing, I felt like one of Carrie's married friends whom she'd lost touch with because, well, they were ordinary as shit. I certainly didn't want anyone to think of me this way. After all, I was supposed to be the fun city girl!

City or no city, I still aspired to be the fun, lively, and interesting one who had news to share, stories to tell, and people to see. I wanted to always look fabulous and chic, with or without kids. But my life was going in a different direction, and I didn't hate it.

I mean, I was tired. So tired. And I loved yoga pants. And oversized sweaters. And oh my fucking god, did I hate wearing bras. Putting on makeup every day? No, thank you. I went from budgeting extra time in my mornings to put on makeup to making extra time for my skincare routine. If the only way to live the extraordinary social life I desired was to put on a full face of makeup every morning, I would admit defeat to this lifestyle immediately. Add having to wear a bra all the time into the mix, and I would run screaming.

What was so wrong with having a social life that was good . . . enough? I wondered. What was so wrong with striving for that sweet balance between being social and being anti-social? After all, it's not like I didn't have a social life at all. I got together with friends multiple times each month.

My problem was that these get-togethers were not as frequent and *fun* as they used to be—and I figured I needed that *fun* in my life to prove to myself that my social life was *not* unimpressive.

What I ended up learning proved me wrong.

I had this friend, Amy, whose social life was like that of a real-life Carrie Bradshaw. Everyone loved her and wanted to hang out with her, and she somehow found time for everyone. Everything about her social calendar seemed impressive, from the constant plans with people to the lavish excursions to the fact that she had the energy not only to do it all, but also to find time to make the plans in the first place.

> What was so wrong with striving for that sweet balance between being social and being anti-social?

So, in my pursuit of a fun and exciting night out, who was I going to call? Obviously, her.

It was a Saturday, and I had just gotten out of the shower. I grabbed my phone and walked into my bedroom, ready to engage in my post-shower ritual of sitting on my bed nude with a towel on my head while scrolling through my phone. Sometime during my scroll, I decided to text her to see if she was around. It was a long shot with the busy schedule I assumed she had, but I was bored and craving that *fun*. It was worth a try.

To my surprise, she was around and free, so we made plans. Dinner, drinks, and the classic "see-where-the-night-takes-us." If this were anyone else, there would be an 85 percent chance that the night would take us home, but with Amy, I had no fucking idea where the night would take me, and I was excited to find out.

With an exciting night now on the horizon, I worked up the energy to get off my bed, put on makeup, and blow dry my hair, a task I hate doing—and also the main reason I try to avoid showering.

Once this was done, it was time for the outfit selection, another ritual of mine. I like to compare this one to a full season of *The Bachelor*. In this act, I try on many different outfits, finding things I like and dislike about most, while outright eliminating others. After making some hard choices, I end up selecting a few favorites for "hometown dates," a.k.a. I send pictures of myself in them to friends and family. Then, my selection finally commences in The Final Rose ceremony, where I try on my favorite two outfits again before picking one and praying I made the right choice in such a small amount of time.

That night, I ended up choosing an old favorite: a black, long-sleeve, oversized, silky top with leather leggings and black Sam Edelman booties.

After taking twenty-four selfies in the hopes of taking one in which I actually liked the way I looked (I did not), I glanced over at the clock and saw I was supposed to be at the restaurant in twenty minutes. Fuck. I ordered an Uber, grabbed my bag, and ran out the door to greet my driver.

I entered the restaurant like a category-four hurricane, smiling at the hostess as I rushed to the bar at the end of the room. From afar, I saw Amy sitting, drinking white wine, and talking to a middle-aged man next to her. I wondered if she'd brought this man, until he got up and left.

"Hey!" I said to her as I threw my bag and leather jacket on the bar and hopped up on the stool next to her.

"Hi!" she said back. We hugged. Ah, the hug. Why is it that every time I say hello to a friend and goodbye to a friend, we hug? I don't want to hate on hugs here, but I do think that the hugging has gotten a little excessive. Like, hugs have kind of lost all meaning to me now, and this is bad for many reasons. The other week after drinks with co-workers, I started hugging people goodbye out of habit, and one gave me a look like I was insane. I mean, what's next? I go into work and start hugging people hello? It's not right. But I digress. Back to my night with Amy.

"Did you know him?" I asked, grabbing the menu in front of me.

"No, he was just some dude who was sitting here." See, everyone, even random-ass people, love Amy. I, on the other hand, scare people by hugging them.

Over appetizers and wine, Amy and I caught up on each other's lives. She told me about all the great dates she had gone on recently, and I told her about the mediocre amount of weddings I had coming up that summer. She told me about her impressive upcoming trip to Europe, and I told her about the time my unimpressive self tripped walking outside. She told me about the exceptional promotion she just got at work, and I avoided telling her anything about my unexceptional job, because it just wasn't very interesting.

"So, what do you want to do after this?" I asked, hoping she would already have the most perfect bar in mind that I had never even heard of because that's how cool it was.

"I have no idea. What do you think?"

"You're the one who still goes out all the time," I laughed. "Not me. I don't know what's fun anymore."

"I just go to restaurant bars like this. I haven't been *out* out in a while. You go out more than me."

"Oh," I replied, shocked that Amy wasn't living the extraordinary Carrie Bradshaw life I thought she was.

We went back and forth, debating what to do next, before we lost all hope and decided to ask my two younger brothers what was up. Lo and behold, they were at a club with their friends about a quarter of a mile from where we were. I showed Amy the text, and we exchanged grins before shrugging our shoulders and deciding to go.

I would like to take a moment to thank alcohol for making all of this possible. Now, back to our regularly scheduled programming.

After we paid the bill, we threw on our jackets and started walking to the club. A minute after we got outside, I began to panic. Why in the world did I agree to go to a club? I was tired and full from eating. I also didn't want to wait in a line. All clubs have lines. Was getting through a line the secret to having an impressive social life? Because if so, I was really going to have to reevaluate my desire to have one.

We finally got to the club, and a line was visible down the street.

Amy saw the horror on my face. "Let's just wait in the line for a few minutes," she said. "We made it this far. And this could be hilarious," she said, nodding her head toward a parade of young girls walking by in stomach-baring crop tops.

"Okay," I agreed, even though I was still in my light jacket, unprepared for this weather. How those girls were sporting bare stomachs, I had no idea. I was freezing, and all parts of my body were covered except my face and hands.

Luckily, the line moved quickly. After we paid the $20 to get in and had smiley faces stamped on our left hands, we walked inside. I could hear the music getting louder and the bass getting stronger as we walked down the hallway into the room with the giant dance floor. My head already hurt.

"This looks insane," I said to Amy.

"What?" she yelled over the music.

"Never mind," I said back.

"What?" she yelled again.

I was suddenly remembering why I didn't like living this lifestyle anymore.

My brothers and their friends saw us and came running over. As we were saying hello, there was a loud pop, and confetti fell from the ceiling. People screamed. I wondered why I had gotten myself into this mess, while trying to make out what the club patrons around me looked like between strobe-light flashes.

"I'm going to get a drink," Amy screamed. "Do you want one?"

I debated saying yes for about a second, until I felt my head starting to spin. "I'm all set."

"Okay," she shrugged before walking away, her impressive amount of energy effortlessly fitting in with the younger crowd.

I was left standing with my two younger brothers and their friends, tired, head now pounding. I wanted nothing more than to go home, get into bed, and fall asleep.

While standing there, awkwardly swaying my body to the music, not speaking because the music was too loud to talk over, a man walked up and asked me to dance. I shook my head no, then walked around to the other side of the circle. My brothers saw this, glanced at each other, and in their drunken stupor started yelling at this man for asking me to dance.

As I watched them yell at this random guy, I debated leaving. Amy still hadn't come back. She had probably met someone at the bar. I was now alone, standing in the middle of a club I didn't want to be at, full of people four to seven years younger than me, watching a bunch of grown men yell at each other. I decided it was time to go. I took out my phone to order an Uber home and walked toward the bar to find Amy. Just as expected, she was laughing and chatting with people at the bar. Instead of interrupting, I opted to text her I was leaving as I walked into the front hallway of the bar to wait for my ride.

"Lame," she responded.

I got in the backseat of the Uber and was greeted by a talkative driver. I tried looking busy on my phone to avoid the conversation, but it did not work. By the time we arrived outside my apartment, I knew all the names and birth dates of the man's four children, where his wife had grown up and what she did for work, and the theme of his high school senior prom. Uber rides are either like this or completely silent. They literally have no in-between, you guys.

"This is good," I told him when we were pulled up outside my apartment. "Good luck with everything!" I said to my new friend before shutting the door.

As he drove away, I started fumbling around in my bag. My keys. I couldn't find my keys. I started panicking.

I called Dan, who was still just my boyfriend at this point, hoping he was still awake and would let me in. No answer. I called again. And again. And again. And again. No answer.

I went to the front entrance of my building and dialed the code to get in, which was connected to Dan's phone (go figure). No answer. I tried opening the front door and picking at the lock, but who was I kidding? I had no idea how to do this.

All I wanted was to go inside the door in front of me so I could walk up the stairs to my apartment, go inside, go to the bathroom, take off my bra, and go to bed. All I needed was for Dan to answer his fucking phone so I could go inside. It's not like he could be in such a deep sleep that he wouldn't wake up to one of my six hundred phone calls. That would be impossible. Right?

I called Dan again. In fact, I called him thirty-six times in a row, all resulting in his stupid voicemail message, which I now knew by heart. I started crying.

At that point, it was 2 a.m. I had to pee, and my bladder pressure was getting worse. That's when I decided to retreat into my car. People always ask me why I keep my car keys separate from my apartment keys. I wasn't sure before, but now I tell them it's for this reason: in case I lock myself out of my home and need a place to go temporarily.

I got into the front seat of my Honda CR-V, locked the doors, and shifted the seat back so I could lie down, ensuring that no one would see me (not that there was anyone in the parking lot in back of my apartment, but you never know who could emerge, and I was not taking any chances). Then, I proceeded to keep calling Dan, each time receiving no answer, while swimming my legs, manically trying to fight off the urge to pee.

At this point, I was cold. Remember, all I had with me was my fucking light jacket. I turned on the car to start the heat. Sitting there, I started wondering if this was safe. I was so tired. I just wanted to take a little catnap until Dan finally answered his phone so I could go inside, but if I did would I get carbon monoxide poisoning? I rolled down one of the windows a tiny bit to let in some air and started googling "Can you die from sleeping in a running car?"

Just after this, around 3 a.m., I got a text from my brother. "Where are you? Come over."

I responded: "I'm locked out and hiding in my car. Dan won't answer his phone to let me in. I just want to go inside."

Then, Amy called. I answered. "Hello," I said, sniffling slightly, trying to hide the fact that I'd been sitting in my car crying while trying to both not die and not pee my pants.

"What the fuck are you doing? Get out of your car and come to your brother's. Call an Uber," Amy said.

"No, no, I'm good. Dan's going to answer his phone soon."

"No, he's not," she spoke over what sounded like tons of people in the background.

"Wait, why are you at my brother's apartment?" I asked.

"I have no idea," she said.

"Is someone playing the guitar?" I asked.

"Yeah, there's tons of people here. Just come."

But I didn't want to go there. In fact, I didn't want to go anywhere except into my fucking apartment. I said goodbye and hung up the phone, now kicking my feet together like a kid driving up to the entrance of Disney World. I couldn't hold it in much longer. I debated peeing my pants, but I couldn't do that. That would get on the seats. I couldn't pee on the seats. But the bladder pressure was getting worse. I had to go. I had to find a way.

I made a round of calls to Dan again. No answer.

"FUCKING DAN," I yelled to myself, blaming him for my irresponsible choice to go out without my apartment keys and drinking to the point where I had to pee every three minutes.

Luckily, I had an idea. I had to get to the trunk. I didn't want to get out of the car, because I was still afraid of being seen, so I hopped over the seats, rolled into the trunk, and saw what I was looking for: a recyclable Wegmans grocery bag and a beach towel—my tickets to sweet release.

It was there in that trunk that I pulled down my leather leggings and peed into the Wegmans bag, wiping myself with the beach towel after. Then, I pulled back up my leggings and made my way back to the driver's seat.

Once I was up there, I started calling Dan again, crying more and more each time he did not answer. Around 4 a.m., I didn't know if I would be able to stay awake much longer. I tried nodding off, but I was too scared someone would see me sleeping in my car and try to break in to kill me. So, between nod offs, I would call Dan.

Finally, around 5:30 a.m., when the sun was in the process of coming up, I got a phone call. It was Dan.

"Hello," I said into the phone, my voice full of fire, rage, and relief. However, after I'd spent three seconds celebrating the fact that Dan was not dead in our apartment and was in fact sleeping through my two hundred phone calls, it was just full of fire and rage.

"I'm so sorry," he said, referring to the one hundred angry text messages I'd sent him, most in all-caps, asking him WHY THE FUCK HE WASN'T ANSWERING HIS PHONE and WHY THE FUCK HE WAS DOING THIS TO ME. "I'm coming outside."

I did not say a word. I just hung up the phone in anticipation of his arrival.

He walked up to the car, opened the door, took one sniff, and asked if I smelt something funny.

"Yes. I peed in the trunk in a Wegmans bag," I said as I got out of the car.

He looked at me funny.

We opened the trunk, grabbed the Wegmans bag and beach towel, and threw both out in the trash on our walk to the front door.

When we got inside our apartment, I immediately took off my bra and, of course, went to the bathroom. As I got into bed, Dan asked, "Was it at least a fun night?"

"What is *fun*?" I responded, before telling him not to talk to me for twenty-four hours. I then went to bed.

That night, I learned that the word *fun* has a different meaning for everyone. *Fun* is not something you can force. It's not a thing. It's a feeling, and it's different for literally anyone. It can even be different for you depending on the day. I tried to force *fun* on myself based on the idea that fun nights out were what I used to experience, and meh nights out were what I was experiencing now. What I didn't realize is that meh was fun for me now.

My social life had been good enough all along. It didn't need to be extraordinary. I didn't need a calendar jam-packed with get-togethers and events like Carrie Bradshaw's, or even Amy's. I was doing fine enough.

NOW, I WANT to share the most important things I learned so you, too, can embrace your good-enough social life.

* **Everyone has a different idea of average when it comes to their social life, making greatness yours to define.** When it comes down to it, a social life is like a bikini body. If you've got a body in a bikini, you've got a bikini body. If you've got a life and you're being social, you have a social life. You don't need to go to clubs or bars or even restaurants to have a social life. You don't even have to host or attend dinner parties. After all, there is *no* set way a social life should look. You can live your social life however the fuck you want to live it, and you can define greatness however the fuck you want to define it. Oh, and you can change your mind about the things you want and enjoy, too.

  I didn't realize this until it was too late, leading to my peeing in a Wegmans bag in the trunk of a car. Different from what I thought, it wasn't that I wasn't *fun* anymore, and it wasn't that my social life was un-impressive. It was that I had changed. It was that my idea of *fun* and *impressive* had changed. I had set a definition of "greatness" years ago, and I didn't re-alize that I could change it. But I could, and I did. And now my "greatness" involves a happy medium of doing nothing on the couch with no one else and getting together with friends.

* **Having an impressive social life can be a burden.** The social lives featured on television shows like *Sex and the City* and *Friends,* where grown adults always have the time and energy to hang out, are unrealistic and also kind of terrifying.

Unrealistic because in real life, your friends prob-ably don't live in such close proximity to you. People are busy with their own shit, and you're busy with yours. It's hard to nail a time down on one person's calendar, never mind getting a bunch of people to-gether. Imagine forcing yourself to do this every sin-gle day, or even a few times a week. I would get so stressed, I would probably become one gigantic hive.

You are also not a robot (right?), so chances are you get tired. I mean, I would personally never have the energy to go out to a bar on a weeknight after I was already in bed for the night like Carrie did on *Sex and the City,* but maybe that's just me.

* **With a mediocre social life, you get the best of both worlds.** This is where the happy medium thrives, my friends. As an average human, sometimes you want to do things and sometimes you don't. Well, guess what? When you accept your social life as good enough, you'll be able to embrace both the nights spent on your couch AND the nights out with friends.

   You won't hate on the couch and blame its down-filled cushions for keeping you from having an impressive social life. Nor will you hate on your friends for not being exciting enough or not wanting to do exceptional things all the time. You'll be happy with the nights in and happy with the nights out, no matter how average they feel. Isn't that what it's all about, anyway? Being happy? Find your happy medium, people, and never let it go!

* **You're not socially unimpressive if you're doing shit you enjoy doing.** Your social life (and your life in general) shouldn't look like anything except whatever you want it to look like, and *no one* should judge you for that. And if you need to have a night out during which you get locked out of your apartment and pee in your car to figure out what you want, by all means do it. The relief that comes from accepting yourself.for who you are is just as sweet as the relief that results from peeing after holding it in for three hours. I promise.

Canceling Plans: A Guide for People with Second-Rate Social Skills

BECAUSE YOU DON'T WANT TO GO. AND NEITHER DO THEY.

Well, this is awkward. You made plans a month and a half ago to get drinks after work on a Tuesday with an old friend you ran into at the grocery store. After chatting about how *good* it was to see each other, you set a date and time for a formal catch-up session. You then put the plans into the calendar on your phone, said goodbye, and went on your merry way to scan the fuck out of all the bananas (please don't tell me I'm the only one who spends thirty-five minutes checking out every inch of bananas before buying them; this is how I spend 75 percent of my time in the grocery store).

With only a few days left until the event, you start to panic. Why did you make these plans? What were you thinking? It's a Tuesday, for god's sake. If you're going to skip a Tuesday workout, you'd really prefer to lean in to your average lifestyle and watch TV on the couch all night sans bra. This isn't even plans with a friend. It's plans with an acquaintance. How can you get out of this? Maybe you will get a stomach bug. Or pneumonia. Or mono. You cough. Hmm, not raspy enough. You open all the windows in your home and strip down to your underwear. It is mid-January and below freezing outside. Now you will at least have a chance of becoming sick and having to cancel.

Okay, I'm just kidding. You wouldn't go that far. Or would you?

Now it's Tuesday. You wake up to the sound of pouring rain hitting the ground outside. It's dark, and you have zero interest in getting out of bed to go to work, never mind doing something after work. But, FUCK, that's right. You have to do something after work. You have plans, and your social skills are not advanced enough to find an easy way out of them.

The weather app on your phone says it's going to be miserable all day, just like you will be if you can't find a way out of these damn plans. You could text the person and say you woke up sick and need to cancel. You could text the person and say something came up with your kids or your dog or your partner or your home and you need to cancel. You could text the person and say you are allergic to rain and will unfortunately have to reschedule these plans to another day, but no—you don't want to reschedule! You just want to *cancel*. Also, you are not allergic to rain, but that doesn't matter.

You end up not getting anything done at work all day because you are too busy stressing about what to do. You don't want to get caught in a lie. You don't want to get labeled as a flake. You don't want word to get out that you're an evil plan canceler, because what if no one makes plans with you ever again? But then how do you cancel?

Then, around 4 p.m., you get a text.

"Hey! So sorry, but something came up and I need to cancel tonight. Sorry this is so last minute!"

Are you fucking kidding?

After a minute of being angry at the lack of effort that went into this plan-cancellation text (like, where is the excuse?!?!? Huh, HUH?), you suddenly blast off through the roof of your office building, tap the moon, and then plummet back into your desk chair.

NOW YOU CAN GO HOME AFTER WORK AND TAKE OFF YOUR BRA!

Or, NOW YOU CAN GO WORK OUT, BUT YOU'RE NOT GOING TO!

Hell, maybe you'll even pop open a bottle of wine tonight to celebrate.

Your average plans were averagely cancelled.

Hal-le-fucking-lujah.

The end.

———

NOW, LET'S DISCUSS.

Why were you so afraid to cancel these plans from the beginning? Clearly this person wanted to cancel too. Even if they were genuinely excited about these plans and something really did come up last minute, they didn't value your plans enough to tell you what the thing was that came up. They didn't even ask to reschedule.

Basically, you were both on the same page here. Neither one of you wanted to go.

To avoid this in the future, you could avoid making plans with people you have no interest in making plans with. But that's not going to stop you from wanting to cancel plans. Hell, I cancel plans all the time. I do so with my best friends and my husband. I even cancel plans with myself. Let's take today, for example. I was supposed to go to barre class at 5:30 p.m., but I panicked last minute and cancelled it, eating the $15 late cancellation fee. Like, that is how bad I am. Even if humans charged a $15 late cancellation fee for plans, I would absolutely, 100 percent still pay it to cancel because I am a subpar human, and sometimes I just don't want to do shit, okay?

But I should be clear. I do not always cancel plans, even if I want to. Like, if I have plans to go to someone's wedding, I don't bail last minute just because I don't want to be around the other humans going to the wedding. I suck it up and go because I already RSVPed. I'm not *that* much of an asshole. Also, open bars are a gift.

This is why I have created a guide to canceling plans last minute so all of us average folk can avoid the anxiety that comes with having to do shit you said you would do that you don't want to do anymore. Happy canceling!

HOW TO CANCEL PLANS LAST MINUTE
WITHOUT BEING AN ASSHOLE

Tier Key

1. These are cardinal plans, meaning they are above average (i.e., important). When you RSVPed yes, money was spent with the idea that you would be there. Excellent excuses necessary.

2. These are right below cardinal plans, but not as important, meaning these plans are kind of like you: they're average. They may be worth forcing yourself off the couch to go, OR they may not be. Excellent excuses encouraged.

3. In the grand scheme of things, these plans really don't matter, but if you value your friendships, you may not want to throw these plans away. Good excuses necessary to maintain friendships.

4. These plans don't need excuses. If you don't want to go last minute, don't go. At the end of the day, no one will be angry with you for not going. Just being honest here.

Plans	Where on the Tier?	Why?	Acceptable Excuses for Last-Minute Cancelling:
Wedding	1	You shouldn't RSVP yes to a wedding and not show up. People paid for your presence. Have respect.	Dead relative, nonstop explosive diarrhea, emergency surgery, pink eye
Other Milestone Event (Baby Shower, Graduation, Bachelorette Party, Kids' Dance Recital, Reunion)	2	If it involved a headcount, you should go if you RSVPed yes. Not as much money, if any, was probably spent on you as a wedding, but show respect.	Family emergency, extreme stomach pain, surgery, cancelled babysitter if you can't bring kids, car issues, pink eye
Child's Birthday	2	It's a kid's birthday! What kind of person RSVPs to a child's party and doesn't show up?	Anything that could be contagious, family emergency, stomach issues, car issues
Date	2	If this is a first date or close to it, you have to be okay with not seeing this person again. Know the risks.	Flu, stomach issues, family emergency, "work thing"
Work Event	2	You should always TRY to go to the work event to network and mingle, but you can't go to all of them.	Stomach issues, something contagious if you're planning to skip the work day too, family emergency, your kids, your dog
Birthday Dinner	3	Birthdays happen every year, so they aren't THAT important, but if plans with a few people were made with you included, try to suck it up and go.	Stomach issues, something contagious, cancelled babysitter, sick kid, stuck at work
Dinner Party	3	If ingredients were purchased and a menu was created with your seat in mind, don't be a dick. Try to go if you can.	Stomach issues, something contagious, cancelled babysitter, sick kid, stuck at work
Party Thrown by Friend	3	A party isn't THAT big of a deal, but if your friend is counting on you being there, at least try to make an appearance.	Stomach issues, something contagious, cancelled babysitter, sick kid

Plans	Where on the Tier?	Why?	Acceptable Excuses for Last-Minute Cancelling:
ANYTHING with One Friend	3	If you cancel on this person, their day or night will be cancelled as well since you had one-on-one plans. Remember that.	Stomach issues, something probably contagious, family thing, sick kid
Party Thrown by Acquaintance	4	It doesn't matter if you go.	You don't need an excuse. You can't make it anymore. They won't care. They barely know you.
Night out or Night in with Friends	4	It doesn't matter if you go.	You don't need an excuse. Just say you don't feel like going. Don't ignore texts and pretend you fell asleep the next day. Just say you changed your mind. They'll get over it.
Dinner, Drinks, or Coffee with an Acquaintance	4	IT DOESN'T MATTER IF YOU GO. But you probably won't hang out with this person again so tread lightly.	You don't need an excuse, but maybe say you're not feeling well. Just so they don't think you're an asshole. You never know if you'll want to make plans with them again one day.

THE
**I'M HAPPY WITH
THE WAY I LOOK!**
AWARD

3

NO ONE IS JUDGING YOUR AVERAGE BODY–EXCEPT YOU

. . . and other thoughts about striving for healthy happy mediums

When Our Bodies Are Average and Our Shame Is Supreme

"When are you due?" the woman at the cash register eagerly asked after telling me how much I owed.

I looked at her funny before glancing down at the six small boxes of pizza towering over my hands. I took one hand away for a second to grab the cash out of my pocket, praying the boxes would not tumble to the ground.

As I fumbled through the disorganized mess of credit cards, gift cards, and old receipts, looking for the money my dad had given me to pay for all of this pizza, I wondered what the woman at the register meant. When am I due? When am I due home with these pizzas so my family doesn't starve? When am I due back to college?

"Sorry, I'm such a mess," I said while handing the money I had rounded up to the cashier.

I then placed my free hand back under the pizza box tower and noticed that the bottom box had been resting on top of my stomach. It was resting. It almost looked like as if I could be—pregnant.

The cashier was still smiling at me, waiting for an answer to her original question.

"Oh, I'm not—" I mumbled under my breath, "not—"

I couldn't get the words out.

She handed me back my change, still smiling, but now with a slight hint of confusion on her face. I immediately turned around and made a dash to the exit. I did not look up from the pizza boxes to see who was around me. To see who might have heard our conversation. To see who might now think I was pregnant.

At the time, I was eighteen years old and home from college for winter break. Sure, I had gained some weight that first semester of my freshman year (the dining hall had french fries every single night, give me a break), but I sure as hell wasn't pregnant. After all, I was still a virgin. I was just wearing a shirt that wasn't the most flattering for my average frame, and I guess it made my belly pooch show, which is an extremely average thing to have if we're being honest here, which we are. Okay, back to me.

I was never thin. Unlike my mom, who wore crop tops as a teenager (I've seen photo evidence), I was blessed with genes from my dad's side of the family, meaning that from the moment I came out of the womb, I had a slow metabolism and a soft spot for food. French fries, chicken nuggets, Diet Pepsi, bagels, pizza, Cheez-Its, the list goes on. Growing up, even when I convinced my mom I was eating healthy by picking at vegetables during dinner, I would sneak bags of chips into my room at night, hiding the evidence under my bed (I thought she would never find the bags there; spoiler alert: she did).

I was also never unhealthily overweight. Sure, I got the yearly lecture at the doctor's office during my physical about being "overweight" or sometimes even "obese" according to the BMI scale, but I had picked up on the fact that the system was bullshit at a very young age. If I, a 5'2" teenager with a muscular build who could fit into the undersized clothing from Hollister, was being told I was obese, what the fuck were they telling people bigger than I was?

This was one of the many reasons I never felt like I could like my average body. The other reasons:

* I was on a dance team for the majority of my youth, meaning I spent multiple hours each week prancing around in a leotard and tights in a room full of skin,

bones, and mirrors. Compared to the rest of the girls, my weight was by no means average, and with every second spent staring at myself in the mirror next to all of them, I became more and more self-conscious about my stomach and thighs.

* I had a full-length mirror in my bedroom at home, so my self-conscious spiral would continue after dance. There, I would stand naked in front of my mirror, turning to the side and sucking in my stomach to see what I would look like if I were smaller.

* I read magazines and watched television. Rarely did those things feature women without six packs, and when they did, it was usually someone owning their plus-size frame. I was neither of those things, so where the fuck did average bodies like mine fit in?

* As a teen, I wore sizes 10, 12, large, and extra-large. These sizes are not big. They are just average. But for some reason, two of them are literally named large and EXTRA large. Just like our BMI scale, our clothing-size scale is all fucked up. Like, the fact that a clothing size named "extra-large" is a size before plus-size territory is insane. It's like we are pressuring people to develop warped views of their bodies (or at least this is what happened to me).

* In high school and college, I was a cheerleader. If you were not also a cheerleader, I know what you're thinking. You're picturing the stereotypical American cheerleader—blonde, thin, and pretty—just like society has trained you to do. I was none of that. But I was good at cheerleading. My movements were sharp as fuck, and my thighs made me a strong-as-shit base for stunting. However, not looking "the part" made me quite self-conscious.

* I gained about fifteen pounds during my first semester of college, and came home to a cashier at a pizza place asking me when my baby was due.

When I got home with the pizzas that day, I dropped them on the kitchen counter, ran up to my bedroom, shut the door, and marched right over to my full-length mirror. I turned to the side and saw it—or at least I think I saw it: a belly that resembled one of a woman who was about four to five months pregnant. I then tore off my clothes and stared at my body again. I hated it. I hated how average it was. I hated my stomach. I hated my love handles. I hated my thighs.

I walked into my bathroom and stepped on the scale. 183 pounds. Just two years before, I had weighed thirty pounds less.

Looking back up at myself in the mirror, tears started forming in my eyes. That was it. I didn't want to have an average body anymore. I wanted to have a great body. For some reason, I figured changing my body would change my life. That suddenly men would be attracted to me. That a smaller frame would entice more people to be my friend. That a better-than-average body would make me better-than-average at everything else. Was I right? Not in the fucking least. But was I motivated to make a change because of this flawed thought process? Absolutely.

My plan to lose weight at first was 80 percent giving up french fries and pizza and 20 percent counting calories and working out. I wish I could say that was a joke, but it wasn't. It took a lot to give up french fries and pizza.

Although the plan was working and I was losing about one to two pounds per week, after a few months, I became impatient. This caused me to crack down on my calorie consumption.

Unhealthily embracing the motto "hunger passes," I would force myself to wait to eat meals until whenever I was hungry for a snack. When I was out socializing, I would limit myself to minimal drinks and junk food. I remember one night that summer I was at a work outing and pizza was the only option for dinner. I was starving, so I had to eat it, but I didn't let myself have more than one slice. It didn't matter how hungry I was. I couldn't fuck up while in pursuit of a better-than-average body.

Toward the end of that summer, all together I was down about fifteen pounds. Back to a cool 168. The in-between of sizes 8 and 12, depending on where you're shopping. While

I knew I looked smaller, I also knew I was still a very average weight. And because of this, there was no way I was going to embrace my progress thus far.

A few days before heading back to college for the fall of my sophomore year, some of my high school girl friends invited me to dinner at The Cheesecake Factory. I debated whether or not I should go. I wouldn't be home until winter break, and I wanted to see them one last time before then, but I had come so far with my diet—and I still had a long way to go (or so I thought).

My previous experience of going to The Cheesecake Factory involved binging on the hot bread served before dinner (both the brown bread and the baguette bread) and then ordering a cheeseburger and fries. I knew I could just order a salad instead and, you know, not eat the free bread, but did I have the willpower to avoid it?

At this point, I was becoming fully aware that I had gotten a little carried away with the dieting. My daily calorie intake was becoming a topic in all of my conversations, and my workout plans were taking precedence over everything and everyone else in my life. And now I was debating not saying goodbye to friends I wouldn't see for four months because I was afraid of free bread? What was happening to me? I had to go to this dinner. I had been so good for the six months prior, ever since being asked the "When are you due?" question. What damage could one night do?

I got to the restaurant and sat down next to the other girls. While we reminisced about the summer and talked about our upcoming semesters, I could not stop thinking about how I was going to have to avoid the bread. As soon as the waiter came over and dropped the bread basket on our table, each of the girls took a piece. I sat there, staring at them, my mouth watering, reminding myself over and over that I shouldn't take one. Why not, though, I wondered. Was one piece of bread really going to mess up my entire diet? I ended up taking a slice, which lead to another slice, and another one after that . . . and then an order of french fries with my salad.

After dinner, I went home and booked it to my bathroom. Disgusted with myself, I took off my clothes and stepped on the scale to see just how bad the damage was. Apparently, I had gained four pounds since that morning. I debated vomiting the entire meal away. I had never made myself throw up before, though. I didn't know how to do it—or if I even could.

I looked at the toilet, looked at the scale, and looked in the mirror. I had to do it. I had to make myself throw up. I turned on the faucet, kneeled down in front of the toilet, stuck two fingers down my throat, and waited until remnants of the bread, french fries, and salad came up and fell into the toilet. After purging four times, my nose hurt like hell and my eyes were watering like never before. I flushed the toilet, got up, and walked back over to the scale. I had lost two pounds. It was like I had never gone out to eat. It had worked.

I promised myself I would never do that again. That it was a one-time thing. I didn't have an eating disorder. I was fine. I had been healthy about losing weight until now. I was going to go back to school and continue my diet until I was satisfied with my weight. Until I looked better than average. I was fine.

Back at school, everyone I came in contact with complimented my weight loss.

"Oh, thanks, but I know I don't *really* look great yet. You just wait and see!" I would tell them, unable to accept any admiration. At least not yet. Not while my body was still average.

With every pound lost, I felt like I was only becoming more average. I was blending in more with the crowds, not standing out. Rarely was I the girl to whom guys flocked at parties. No. Those were my friends with better bodies, or at least I had convinced myself of this. I figured I needed to look great to be great, but no matter how I looked, I always seemed to find a new flaw in the mirror to obsess over: armpit fat, chubby cheeks, rolls in my back. I just could not let myself win.

Losing more weight became a struggle at school. It was hard to find healthy food in the dining hall, and my friends wanted to go out all the time. *Staying in* was not a term in my vocabulary during college (I suffered from a severe case of FOMO, also known as SFOMO), so if friends were going out, I went out too, meaning I drank. And where there was me and booze, there was pizza.

A few weeks into the semester, I weighed myself after a night out to find the same number I had seen every day since leaving for school. While I was trying to be as good as possible, the unhealthy nights spent with booze and pizza offset the healthy ones. I had hit a plateau, and I wasn't sure what to do.

I didn't want to stop going out. Socializing was my favorite thing to do. I also didn't want to start eating less. Some people can go through life eating modest amounts of food each day, but not me. Staying under the recommended calorie count every day was hard enough. I watched the tiny girls in the dining hall who barely ate meals, and I thought about how they probably didn't bring just-in-case snacks with them everywhere and how they probably didn't binge eat chips late at night before bed. Is that what it would take for me to not be average? To stop giving in to hunger?

The only thing I could think of that would help me start losing weight again was to make myself throw up after eating unhealthy foods. Not all foods. Just unhealthy ones. A few slices of drunken pizza. A big bowl of pasta from a restaurant. Late-night french fries. Any and all alcohol. I figured since I would never really change my average eating habits, this was the only thing that would change my average body. And, of course, I figured this couldn't be considered an eating disorder, because I would only be making myself throw up "on occasion." The most un-average thing about me is that I spent years believing this.

During those years, I worked out, ate healthy, and threw up anything too unhealthy that I put in my body. My weight fluctuated between 165 pounds and, my very lowest, 145 pounds. But no matter how much I weighed, I still only focused on my flaws. Never did I look in the mirror to applaud my waist for looking smaller or my arms for looking toned. I just stood there looking for imperfections. Did my stomach look too big? Could I see rolls? What about back fat? And my thighs—did they look gigantic? Was there a way for them to NOT look gigantic? My face looked bigger than usual too. Was that a double chin?!

I started to wonder if I should be throwing up more. But no. In my mind, that would have made me bulimic. See, I was only throwing up a couple times each year. Plus, I didn't think I was small enough to look like someone who had an eating disorder. I still had an average body. I still wore size 8 and size 10, and I still purchased medium- and large-sized clothes. So, I continued on, until things started to change.

You're probably wondering how things started to change. What got me to realize I was being a complete and total dumbass and embrace my average body for the queen it is? Well, the answer is really short and sweet: confidence.

Let me explain how I found it.

After seven years of the same workout routine filled with treadmill intervals and random weight machines at the gym, I hurt my back and had to take a hiatus from exercising. Because of this, I started gaining weight again, and because of that, I started throwing up what I was eating more often. I felt horrible, and I just couldn't shake the vicious cycle I was in.

Meanwhile, a friend had been trying to convince me to go to the new Pure Barre studio with her. She claimed it would be great for my neck and back because it was low-impact. Desperate for a change and to work out again without getting hurt, I tried the class.

At first, it was hell. Planks for ninety seconds?! An actual thing called "thigh sprints" where it's normal for your legs to shake uncontrollably?! Slowly moving your leg and your seat while in an awkward position and also in 911-worthy pain?! Just kidding about the 911 part . . . or am I? It was hard. But the results were noticeable. After only a few classes, I swear I could feel abs forming underneath my belly fat. I had been doing crunches for years, and I had never felt that before. This class was a game changer.

But it wasn't just a game changer because of the almost-there abs. It was a game changer because it was literally changing my perception of my body. For the first time in my life, I started to feel good about the way I looked.

For years, I had been chasing skinny instead of strong. Sick of being perpetually average, I had wanted my body to

> You're probably wondering what got me to realize I was being a complete and total dumbass and to embrace my average body for the queen it is. The answer is really short and sweet: confidence.

be great, and to me, "great" meant "thin." But I was wrong. So incredibly wrong.

Never in the many years I had spent losing weight did I ever feel as good about my body as I did after I started going to barre class. I felt my body changing, and I became addicted to the results. Instead of searching for flaws in the mirror, I searched for muscle. Instead of obsessing over calories and what I was eating, I started to let myself binge sometimes. The more classes I took, the less I cared about my weight. And the less I cared about my weight, the better I felt.

Finally, for the first time potentially ever, I started to love my average body. I was strong, and I was healthy. The best part: throwing up was in no way a part of my life anymore, and it hasn't been since. I realized I didn't need to throw up to lose weight—and, more importantly, that I didn't need to lose weight at all. My body was average. My body was awesome.

A FEW WEEKS ago, I was getting a pedicure, and the woman cleaning off my feet looked up at me and said "Baby?" as she pointed to my stomach.

Shocked, I looked down at her, down at my stomach, and laughed. "No, no. Not in there."

She awkwardly went back to cleaning off my feet, and I went back to scrolling through Instagram on my phone.

I wondered why this woman thought I was pregnant. My cotton dress was clinging to my stomach, so my belly fat was noticeable a bit. Compared to my toned arms, shoulders, and legs, my stomach pooch may have looked a bit disproportional. After all, I was a petite, 5'2" woman with a stomach that wasn't flat, wearing a cotton dress.

After I got home, I looked at my husband Dan, and asked him, "Do I look pregnant to you?" while turning to the side and holding my arms up.

"No," he replied. "Why?"

I pulled up my dress and asked him again, "Okay, what about now? Doesn't my stomach look like a baby could be in there?"

"No," he said again.

But I insisted as I pulled the dress back down and pulled the cotton to the side to make it tight on my stomach. "What about now?"

"This is a trap," he responded. "You're not pregnant, are you?"

"Ah ha! So I do look pregnant."

"You don't look pregnant. You look fine. Can you stop?"

I stopped asking him questions. But I wasn't done. I walked over to my full-length mirror to examine myself. Maybe I needed to start going to barre class more? Maybe I needed to start really doing Weight Watchers again instead of half-assing it? Maybe I needed to stop drinking wine? Ha, yeah right. Or maybe I actually was pregnant? But in all seriousness, there's no way I would only gain weight in my stomach if I were pregnant. That weight would be every-where, let me tell you.

I started down the rabbit hole of panic.

But then I stopped myself.

When the cashier at the pizza place asked me when I was due twelve years ago, I was a different person. I was self-conscious. I didn't know how to love myself. I let one comment from a stranger make me sick for years, but I wasn't going to do that again. I didn't need to. As a confident, smart woman who rocks curves, muscles, and strong thighs, I love my average body. Why would I want to change it?

If you're still struggling with embracing your average body, let me help. Remind yourself of the following in order to accept your average body for the awesome body that it is:

* **Your average body literally has nothing to do with anything going on in your life.** It's not why certain things are or are not happening in your romantic life. It's not why your career is going a certain way. It's not why you have a certain number of friends. How you *feel* about your average body affects these things. If you feel like shit, or you're self-conscious about the way you appear, people will be less likely to flock to you, and they might not enjoy being around you. However, if you're confident, people will take notice. Confidence is contagious. People are attracted to it. If you feel a certain way about yourself, chances are other people will feel it too.

* **Maintaining a ridiculous physique isn't actually that great.** Preserving a ridiculously in-shape body is honestly a burden. You have to follow absurd diets, basically never skip workouts (even when you're exhausted), and live a very strict life with lots of rules and boundaries. I would rather be average. Wouldn't you?

* **You are not defined by the size of your clothes.** *Large* is not a bad word. Size 10 is not a bad thing. These things are average. Normal. Common. We get so worked up about these things, feeling self-conscious about saying our jeans size out loud in retail stores and branding our wardrobes with certain sizes. But when it comes down to it, who fucking cares? All of our bodies are different, and they're all great in their own way.

* **Being a certain size does not make you great or not great.** A few years ago, I was bridesmaid-dress shopping for a friend's wedding. Out of the six bridesmaids, I was measured for the largest size, a 14, while the rest of the girls were all size 4. I already knew dress shopping would be stressful because I knew I'd have to go two to three sizes up from my usual size, but this made it worse. But why? Why did I assume smaller was greater? I had curves, hips, an ass, big boobs, strong thighs—all great things. When it comes down to it, smaller is not greater. Smaller is just smaller.

* **Everyone feels average sometimes.** Whether you're a size 4, a size 14, or literally any other size, chances are you've felt average before, and chances are you didn't realize that those feelings were average. Maybe you've panicked about taking your cover-up off at the beach because you only feel comfortable in a bathing suit when you're lying down or standing up (and nothing in between). Maybe you've gotten nervous about finishing your meal in front of friends because you don't want them to think you eat too much. Maybe you've worried that people can tell you've gained three pounds. Whatever the case, you're not alone. Duh, you're average. That means you're the norm. That means there's lots of other bodies out there like yours. So, the next time you get all weird about taking your cover-up off at the beach, just remember, we're all in this together. So, please, once and for all—let's stop shaming ourselves for being average.

8 Reasons Life Is Better When You're Mediocre at Being Healthy

The moment I finally started to embrace my average body, I stopped being so hard on myself for average things like craving cheeseburgers, skipping the gym, and eating free food at work. After this, life got much better. After all, our time on this earth is too short to act as our own 24/7 personal trainers. For god's sake, eat the damn cake, people! Or, in my case, the damn pizza. Because, if I'm going to be completely honest here, cake sucks. Pizza, on the other hand, wins, which is a great transition to the following list, which explains why life is infinitely better when you're just okay at being healthy.

1. You don't have to restrain yourself from enjoying the things you crave.

You want the pizza? You can have the pizza. You want the french fries? You can have the french fries. You can also have the cheese and the mac and cheese and the ice cream and the cookies. You can have it all! No, you shouldn't eat yourself into an oblivion of stomach aches (at least not all the time). But you should let yourself breathe every now and then when it comes to the food you eat. As a former chronic dieter, let me tell you, you'll be a lot happier if you let yourself occasionally enjoy the things you want than you would be if you always deny yourself the things you crave.

2. You can freely dabble in the hot bread basket at restaurants without feeling massive amounts of guilt.

As an average healthy person, you get enough nutrients throughout your week that you can feel okay about also eating things that aren't nutritious. So, when that bread basket comes, you can dabble. When someone emails your office with a "free food in the kitchen" message, you can go into that kitchen. And you can do so without feeling like shit. You're good enough at the being healthy thing, and life is infinitely better when you let yourself live with no regrets.

3. You don't stress over whether you should snack when you get hungry.

Life can sometimes seem like a weekly rotation of buying snacks and not buying snacks. When you don't buy snacks, you spend the week wishing you'd bought snacks, and when you do buy snacks, you spend the week wishing you hadn't. But when you finally accept the happy medium of snacking, this vicious cycle goes away, and you end up snacking an average amount per week instead of going nuts one week and being hungry as fuck the next. Well, I guess that is the case, unless your snack of choice is chips and salsa. There is no average amount of snacking that can be done when it comes to this dynamic duo. Like, I am kind of convinced chips and salsa have catnip for people in them? But maybe that's just me?

4. You can have a glass of wine if you want to.

For years, I would often say no to plans that were likely to involve alcohol when I was feeling self-conscious about my body. Whether I was looking at having one glass of wine or a few vodka sodas, I would look in the mirror and say to myself, "Your body does NOT need the calories from alcohol right now . . . or the food you'll crave after drinking it." I would then stay home, feeding my boredom with chips and salsa, and my chronic self-shaming would continue. I was so mean to myself. But why? Nothing was changing, whether I stayed in on a Friday night, went to dinner and drinks with an old friend, or went to the bar with coworkers after work. I also looked fine. The problem was that I wasn't comfortable in my average body. Now that I am, I give myself breaks from my healthy nighttime habits and meet that friend for a drink. A more active social life is a much happier one. I can confirm this.

5. You can skip the gym if it's not calling you.

Some days after work, I just want to go home, sit on the couch, and listen to the TV while refreshing all of my social media feeds on both my MacBook and my phone. In other words, some days I just can't do anything productive, and that's okay. Life is tiring. Sure, I like working out, and yes, I try to be active at least three days a week, but I'm never going to be one of those people who runs ten miles every day or does crunches for five minutes before bed. And if my body-fat percentage is forever mediocre because of that, whatever. I don't need to force myself to do shit I don't want to do in the hopes of becoming an exceptionally healthy person when I'm literally never going to be that person. It does more harm than help.

6. You're okay with letting yourself relax on nights when you don't feel like cooking.

Envious does not even begin to describe how I sometimes feel about people who are able to cook meals every night while simultaneously keeping their homes clean, their social lives active, and their fitness games strong. I can't even manage to cook a real, legitimate dinner two or three nights in a row sometimes, never mind work out and clean too. Instead, when I refrain from cooking, I get takeout. This used to bother me. I wanted to be healthy. I wanted to cook all of my meals! But life kept getting in the way, and that's fine. I was cooking enough, and for my average lifestyle, that was pretty fucking great.

7. You have extra time in your life because you don't fret over setting a rigid, intense diet plan for the week.

Meal planning and prepping is a great idea and all, but the act of doing it every single week can be draining. If I get ambitious and decide to map out my breakfast, lunch, and dinner plans for the following week, it takes me hours to finish. Hours! I have to find recipes, predict what I'll be in the mood for at certain times, and then figure out what makes the most sense based on how much money I want to shell out for groceries and how much time I want to dedicate to cooking. Even when I do this, I never stick to my plans. I get lazy and tired, and the food rots in my fridge, and then I have to throw it out at the end of the week. This is why I try to embrace my averageness and seek a happy medium for meal planning. If I can assign average meal plans and stick to them for half my week, I'm doing good enough.

8. If you're busy and don't have time to plan your meals, you won't starve.

There are always going to be days when you wake up late and have to grab breakfast on the go. There are always going to be weekends when you're too busy doing stuff to go grocery shopping or to think about the days ahead. There are always going to be nights when you didn't eat enough during the day and so you raid the snack cabinet when you get home. All of this is part of being ordinary. There's no reason to be upset if there's a period of time during which you can't do anything healthy at all. It's not like your entire life has been this way so far, and it won't be like this forever. Would you want to be one of those crazy people who doesn't sleep and forces themselves to eat healthy and work out all the time no matter how insane life is? No? You'd rather get your sleep, right? Of course you would. Average people are normal, after all.

Would You Rather:
Care About This Shit or Live Your Life?

A GAME

When it comes to getting ready in the morning, would you rather:

Spend your mornings before work making yourself look exceptional in hopes that other people will view you as a better-than-average person?

OR

Not give a fuck about how meh you'll appear at work and spend your mornings doing shit you want to do, like sleeping, prepping dinner, or cleaning?

When it comes to shopping for jeans, would you rather:

Not ask anyone for help finding your size at a clothing store because you're embarrassed about your size and go home empty-handed?

OR

Not give a fuck about your average body when at a clothing store, get help finding your size from an employee, and go home with a new pair of jeans?

When it comes to eating—or not eating—free food in the office, would you rather:

Smell the sweet scent of a food you love but keep yourself from trying any because you don't want your coworkers to think you're subpar at eating healthy?

OR

Not give a fuck what your coworkers think of your subpar eating habits and treat yourself to whatever it is your nose is lusting after in the kitchen?

When it comes to getting dressed, would you rather:
Complain that you have nothing impressive to wear, even though you have a closet full of clothes, and refuse to leave the house because of this?

OR

Not give a fuck what other people think of your average wardrobe, make do with what you have, and go out into the world to live your life?

When it comes to weighing yourself, would you rather:
Weigh yourself on the scale every day, letting your mood depend on how much it fluctuates, even if you don't feel any different?

OR

Not give a fuck about knowing your ordinary weight and be happy with the way you feel?

When it comes to other people ordering appetizers at restaurants, would you rather:

Not eat the appetizer someone ordered for your table, because you're afraid of what the people there will think of you if you eat too much?

OR

Not give a fuck about what anyone thinks and indulge in this wonderful appetizer because, goddammit, you're good enough at eating healthy. You don't need to be great all the time.

When it comes to ordering entrees at restaurants, would you rather:

Not order french fries at a restaurant even though you really want french fries, because what if everyone else orders salad?

OR

Not give a fuck about what people think of you, give in to the craving you deserve, and order your very own healthy happy-medium meal: a salad with a side of fries?

When it comes to going to the beach,
would you rather:

Panic about taking your cover-up off and awkwardly do it lying down, then spend the rest of your time there refusing to sit up because you can't possibly let other people see you sit in a bathing suit?

OR

Not give a fuck about how unimpressive your body looks in a bathing suit and enjoy your beach trip?

When it comes to posting pictures of yourself online,
would you rather:

Worry about what people will think of your average body when you are debating posting a picture online—and then decide not to post it?

OR

Not give a fuck about what anyone thinks of your average body and post your picture because it's a good-enough fucking picture, and that's all that matters.

*When it comes to socializing with other people,
would you rather:*

Say no to dinner plans because you don't want your average body to gain weight, and thus miss out on what sounded like a fun night?

Or

Not give a fuck about your mediocre body fluctuating a normal amount and spend time with people you love?

THE

I'M GOOD ENOUGH AT LOVE!

AWARD

4

OUR LOVE LIVES ARE PRETTY UNEXCEPTIONAL COMPARED TO THE MOVIES

. . . and other thoughts about ordinary relationships and good-enough love

Relationships: Exceptional Expectations Versus Run-of-the-Mill Reality

MEETING

Exceptional Expectation: You're at a coffee shop, waiting for your latte, when someone bumps into you. You look at them. MY GOD, IT IS LOVE AT FIRST SIGHT. You start talking and realize you have everything in common. They are your dream person. Wedding bells ring in the background. You exchange numbers.

Run-of-the-Mill Reality: You're at a coffee shop, swiping through the weeds of a dating app as you wait for your latte. Everyone starts to look and sound the same. You have no idea what a good fit for you is anymore, so you set up a few dates this week.

FIRST DATE

Exceptional Expectation: You go to a fancy, casual, trendy, intimate restaurant and sit at a corner table away from everyone else. You both have the same taste in food and end up splitting everything. Suddenly, you realize three hours have gone by. You kiss outside the restaurant and decide you will definitely see each other again, then you go your separate ways. Then you skip home because YAY.

Run-of-the-Mill Reality: You go to a crowded or empty restaurant (there is no in-between) and try to find two empty seats next to each other at the bar. You end up hitting it off, but you're kind of drunk, so you're not sure if that was just the wine. You awkwardly kiss goodbye outside the restaurant and decide to see each other again.

STARTING TO REALLY DATE

Exceptional Expectation: You start spending your weekends dining over candlelight and taking long walks in parks holding hands, and during the week you stay at each other's places.

Run-of-the-Mill Reality: You try to make as much time for each other as possible in your busy schedules without coming off as too needy or clingy. You end up seeing each other once or twice a week for the next couple of weeks.

SEX

Exceptional Expectation: Rose petals on a white down comforter. Fireplace going in the background. Temperature not too hot and not too cold, a.k.a. perfect for you to have clothes on AND not on (this is important). Passionate, slow love-making on the decadent comforter, or hot, wild sex before you even reach the bedroom. Either way, you both fall asleep in each other's arms after.

Run-of-the-Mill Reality: You're fooling around on a bed. One of you says, "Do you want to do this?" The other answers, "Yes." Then you take off your clothes, even though it's rather chilly, and you start having sex. There's either a lot of "Do you like this?" and "Do you like that?" or a lot of silence as two sex-strangers try to figure out what's weird and what's not to this new sex partner. Suddenly, it ends. You take turns going to the bathroom to clean up and pee.

MEETING THE FRIENDS

Exceptional Expectation: You bring your new partner to a gathering with friends. Not only does everyone get along with each other, but everyone LOVES your new person. They all pull you aside to tell you so, leaving you so happy that you backflip all the way home after.

Run-of-the-Mill Reality: You bring your new partner to a gathering with friends. They are a bit shy among all these people who know each other already, and stick by your side. Eventually, a few talkative friends make conversation with them. You text your friends after to see what they think, and they all say they liked them. You are relieved, but also still wondering: do they really like your new person, or are they just saying that? Anxiety is a bitch.

MOVING IN TOGETHER

Exceptional Expectation: You move into a beautiful home with many square feet, a wide variety of closets, and a two-sink bathroom. It is always clean, and your home décor game is amazing. You have friends over all the time to entertain, but usually it's just the two of you snuggling on the couch, watching your favorite TV shows.

Run-of-the-Mill Reality: You move into an okay home with a lack of square footage, minimal closet space, and only one bathroom sink. You become disgusted by the person's bathroom habits and annoyed at the lack of compromise when it comes to sharing closet space, but at the end of the day, you love being able to sit on the couch together watching TV, so it's all good.

EATING DINNER

Exceptional Expectation: You make dinner together every night, except the one or two nights a week you go out to a restaurant together.

Run-of-the-Mill Reality: You spend three hours each night going back and forth having the conversation "what do you want for dinner, I don't know, what do you want for dinner"; it eventually becomes too late to make or eat dinner, so you eat snacks or order pizza, or both.

GETTING ENGAGED

Exceptional Expectation: You are alone on a beach together on a beautiful summer day. While walking down the sandy coastline, one of you gets down on a knee and proposes marriage. The one being proposed to had no idea this was coming and starts crying. All of a sudden friends and family start appearing from nowhere, including a professional photographer and a videographer, who got the entire thing on camera.

Run-of-the-Mill Reality: You're on the beach on a mediocre day. You walk to a spot away from the large crowds of people. One of you gets down on a knee and proposes, revealing the ring you picked out together three months ago. The one being proposed to says yes, and you kiss. A group of random people behind you starts clapping. You realize you aren't alone. This is now awkward. You leave to call family and friends, arguing over in what order to call them.

WEDDING PLANNING

Exceptional Expectation: Pure bliss. Happiest time of your life. Everything you want, you get. Everyone is so happy for you all the time.

Run-of-the-Mill Reality: Pure hell. Planning becomes a full-time job, but you both already have full-time jobs. There are too many tiny decisions. Your family is fighting. Everything is expensive, and no one wants to hear you talk about it anymore. You consider eloping, but you don't, because you want the gifts. I mean, really. You do all this for a fucking Dutch oven—and a fun party with all your friends and family—but honestly, is it really worth it? I am not sure. I haven't touched the Dutch oven I got as a wedding gift yet, so I'll have to get back to you on that one.

WEDDING

Exceptional Expectation: Best day of your life. You look the best you've ever looked. You feel the best you've ever felt. Everything goes according to plan. Everyone has a blast.

Run-of-the-Mill Reality: Quickest day of your life. You look good, but not the best you've ever looked. Why does your hair look like that? Why do the flowers look like that? Why are the table numbers on the wrong tables? Most things go according to plan, but other things don't. Everyone still has a blast.

THE HONEYMOON PHASE

Exceptional Expectation: Lots more laughter. Lots more love. Lots more spontaneous sex on kitchen counters (just kidding about the *more* part; we all know this kind of sex doesn't happen in real life, but if it does for you, please tell me your secrets).

Run-of-the-Mill Reality: A bunch of people asking you "How's married life?" and neither of you having an answer, because life is literally the same. Can we please stop asking just-married people this? Thanks.

BUYING A HOME

Exceptional Expectation: You somehow had enough money for a down payment for a home. But not just any home—you bought yourself a nice home in a great area. Said home includes a few thousand square feet, a big-ass backyard, multiple rooms for your potential future children, and a bunch of space for guests. You move in. You go to Pottery Barn. You decorate. You entertain with artfully arranged cheese plates. You love life.

Run-of-the-Mill Reality: There is no reality for this, because it is impossible. I'm just kidding. It's not impossible. There are programs out there for average people who don't have ridiculous amounts of money saved to buy starter homes, and there are also areas where homes aren't insanely priced (I am from Boston, Massachusetts, and home prices are a little nuts here, let me tell you). When you do eventually buy your very average starter home, you lack the funds to decorate it. Instead of Pottery Barn chic, it's, uh, not really chic at all. Just a mediocre home in a mediocre neighborhood. Nothing to see here.

TRAVELING TOGETHER

Exceptional Expectation: Even though you have a mortgage and all of this other stuff to pay for, you still have the funds to travel around the world once or twice or even three times per year. You also each have ample amounts of time off from work to do this, and everyone around you encourages it.

Run-of-the-Mill Reality: You: "There are cheap flights to Aruba right now! We could get a package at an affordable all-inclusive hotel! We haven't gone on vacation in forever. Can we please do this? Oh, wait—I can't take off of work. Never mind."

GETTING PREGNANT

Exceptional Expectation: You plan exactly when you want to start having kids, and then right when that time arrives, you magically get pregnant with your first child. Along with this, you suddenly have the funds to acquire a larger home and all the goods you will need for the baby. The pregnancy is easy and carefree.

Run-of-the-Mill Reality: You keep putting off having kids. Or you try to put it off, and then life decides you're going to start now. Or you decide to start now, and life decides nope, not yet. Or you become unsure if you even want kids.

HAVING COUPLE FRIENDS

Exceptional Expectation: You have a great group of couple friends. Everyone gets along perfectly and wants to hang out all the time. You go to dinners together, take long weekend trips together, and even plan your living situations around being near each other. You know you'll be friends forever, and you know your kids will end up becoming friends too.

Run-of-the-Mill Reality: You have a few couples you hang out with here and there, but for the most part everyone is busy with their own lives and families. You could find new couple friends, but you don't like everyone's spouse enough to pursue more couple friends. Plus, those people are busy anyway. And so are you!

DATE NIGHTS

Exceptional Expectation: Your parents watch the kids whenever you want to go out together.

Run-of-the-Mill Reality: You end up not being able to rely on your parents like you thought you'd be able to. Maybe they don't live near you. Maybe they're busy. Maybe they're not around anymore at all. You can get a babysitter, but you already pay a fortune for daycare, so your date nights are few and far between.

RAISING KIDS

Exceptional Expectation: You have family nights during the week. You go on family outings over the weekend. You watch soccer games and go to dance recitals. There are lots of trips to the zoo.

Run-of-the-Mill Reality: Busy, insane weeknights where each of you drives a kid to their different activities, so you probably never get to do these things together. Busy, insane weekends also spent driving different kids to their different activities. You suffer through soccer games and dance recitals. There are still lots of trips to the zoo.

FAMILY VACATIONS

Exceptional Expectation: You go to your summer beach home for July and August. You invite your couple friends and their families. You also take mid-year trips to Caribbean islands and/or Europe. Your kids are cultured as fuck. You also can still pay your mortgage no problem.

Run-of-the-Mill Reality: You don't have enough money. There is never enough time. You, your spouse, and the kids have completely different schedules. Not to mention, you still have to work. And pay a mortgage. You end up venturing somewhere for a week or two over the summer as a family, but it's honestly stressful as fuck. You hide and drink wine.

25TH ANNIVERSARY

Exceptional Expectation: Your kids throw you a lavish celebration in honor of your milestone. All of your family and friends go. It is like a wedding, but better.

Run-of-the-Mill Reality: Well, if you even make it this far—because, let's face it, a lot of couples won't—your kids will probably be asking you for money instead of using their own to throw you a party. You will have a lack of friends at this point because they'll have fallen deep into the black holes of their own families, like you have. You end up celebrating at a chain restaurant, probably. Help.

RETIREMENT

Exceptional Expectation: You don't have to work anymore, AND you have all this money to blow. Retirement is the best! Finally, you can grow really old together and travel the world and do crazy shit.

Run-of-the-Mill Reality: You actually can't ever retire, sorry. Your 401k can buy you one year of coffees at Starbucks. You guess it's okay because your back is really bad now and you couldn't travel anyway. Oh well.

If the Love Isn't Extraordinary, Can It Still Be Love?

I always assumed that love was this insane thing. That once you found it, once you saw it, you would know right away, and it would take over your body, causing you to sing and dance and be nice to people you hate and so on.

Why did I think this? Because I was fucking told this.

In most movies and television shows, people who are in love are always happy. They whistle. Sometimes they break out into song. Even if they are a normally pissed-off person, when they find love, they change their tune. I hoped that when I found love, I would never be the asshole who randomly whistled in public places, but I did assume that I would be in a good mood for the rest of my life.

In *10 Things I Hate About You*, a guy sang a love song into a microphone for the entire school to see and hear, all so he could prove how extraordinary his "love" was for his person (so what if he was being paid to do it—he believed public serenades equaled love, and due to this, so did I).

In the 1995 classic film *It Takes Two* starring the Olsen twins and Kirstie Alley, we were blessed with this quote: "That can't eat, can't sleep, reach for the stars, over the fence, World Series kind of love." This taught me that I should never settle for a love that was not this extraordinary.

And, of course, in literally every Disney movie, there was always a happily-ever-after ending. Because of this, I thought that once I found my "World Series kind of love" everything after would be a piece of cake (or pizza; I prefer pizza).

When I found love, it wasn't exactly how I imagined it would be. It wasn't always perfect. I wasn't so happy that I had to keep myself from being a whistling-in-public asshole. The closest my significant other came to shouting from the rooftops that he loved me was a couple posts on social media stating that he did in fact love me. It didn't always feel like the World Series. I was able to eat AND sleep, and I was usually far too lazy to reach for any stars or hit a ball over any fence. Oh, and our happily ever after wasn't always happy.

We fought. A lot. About not going on enough dates, about not taking enough vacations, about our apartment being too messy, about my bad money-spending habits, about his eating my stash of protein bars. We literally did not go one week without yelling, screaming, and sometimes even crying about these things. The crying coming mostly from me after realizing he'd eaten my protein bars.

But despite our differences, we loved each other. We made each other happy, and we made each other laugh.

We could talk about anything, and we had fun together. There was really never a time we *didn't* want to be near each other, except of course the time when I had a stomach bug that led to twenty-four hours of horrendously toxic gas being constantly released from my body, and also whenever he clipped his toenails.

In the back of my mind, I wondered if the fact that our love was not the extraordinary love I had imagined meant that it wasn't a great love. There were times it was great, sure, but sometimes it just felt like our love was ordinary, normal, and unimpressive.

Why didn't our love stand out as special when compared to every other couple's love? Why weren't things great for us all the time? What did it mean that we fought? I felt like we had found the perfect happy relationship medium of being good enough. But was good enough *enough* when it came to love? Did love have to be extraordinary for it to really, truly be love?

A week or so before I turned twenty-six, I was out with some friends. Heading out of the bathroom, my eyes grew as I spotted a beautiful man walking in my direction. He was tall, with dark hair and what appeared to be the body of a former high school athlete. He looked as if he could be my Potential Dream Man (let's call him PDM, shall we?).

I quickly looked away to avoid eye contact and continued walking toward my friends. Back at the table, a group of men was now hovering and chatting with them. I looked down at my phone to find it was well after midnight. It was late, and I didn't feel like joining this conversation, so I debated going home. After all, my significant other was at home, and I had no interest in these guys.

As I pulled up the Uber app on my phone, I saw PDM walking toward our table. I froze. He stopped and stood next to the men talking to my friends. Turns out, those were his friends.

Left out of the conversation as well, he spotted me standing on the outside of the circle, smiled, and walked over.

"Hey," he said.

"Hi," I smiled back.

We ended up chatting while our friends continued their conversation beside us. We talked one-on-one until it was closing time and the lights turned on. As everyone started grabbing their jackets, I felt a hand on my back. It was PDM. "Can I get your number?" he asked before taking his hand away.

I looked at him, frozen yet again. Why had I felt something when he touched me? I wasn't supposed to feel *anything* with another guy. After all, I was in love with someone else.

A friend who had been listening tapped my shoulder. "Are you sure you want to do that?" she whispered.

I turned around to answer her question. "It would just be as a friend. It's fine."

By the time I turned back around, ready to answer, PDM was already skeptical. "Why the hesitation?"

"Sorry about that," I said, laughing nervously and taking his phone to put my number in it. We said goodbye and watched the group of guys walk out of the bar while we ordered Ubers.

"Did you really give him your number?" my friend asked.

"No," I said, lying through my teeth to avoid having everyone think I was a horrible human.

We all laughed. I felt my stomach turn. They didn't know the truth, but that did not mean I wasn't a horrible human.

I got in my Uber to head home—back to the apartment I shared with Dan.

When I stepped inside our apartment, all of the lights were off, but the TV was on. I walked in the living room and found Dan fast asleep on the couch. I shook my head. It was shit like this that made me wonder how we were together. I was out drinking with friends, and he was at home falling asleep to a documentary on the History Channel. How was this working? Why did he want *me?* Never mind the fact that we were opposites—I was a bad person. My boyfriend was at home falling asleep on the couch while waiting for me to get home, and I was out giving some random dude my phone number because I felt a weird connection to the way he looked.

I shut the TV off and put a blanket on Dan. I didn't want to wake him. Then, I went into our bedroom to go to sleep. I lay awake for most of that night, thinking about what I had done—and why.

I didn't even know PDM's name. Maybe he would call, I thought. Maybe he would text. Maybe he would reach out tonight or tomorrow, and I could find out if we actually had a connection or if it was just the wine. But wait—what would I do if he reached out? Would I even respond? What if Dan saw? How would I explain it? What was I *thinking?*

Somehow, in the middle all of my manic thoughts, I fell asleep. I woke up the next morning with a pounding head-ache, and the room felt like it was going to start spinning if I moved in the wrong direction.

I grabbed my phone from the night table. No phone calls, no texts. Part of me was relieved. I shouldn't have given my phone number to someone else. I loved Dan. But part of me was also hoping PDM would text. Why? I don't know. Maybe for the validation. Maybe for the boost in confidence that would come from knowing I was still wanted by oth-ers. Or maybe, just maybe, because I thought this could be a sign that my good-enough love was not good enough— and that there could be a greater, more extraordinary love out there waiting for me. Maybe, just maybe, I thought, that someone was PDM.

Dan and I spent the day doing our usual Sunday routine. Grocery shopping. Working out. Making dinner. Watching TV. It was always nice to spend the day together, sure, but this one in particular was nothing special. I wondered what a Sunday would be like with PDM? Would it be this ordi-nary? This mundane?

Lying in bed that night, wrapped in Dan's arms, the thought of PDM kept trying to fight its way into my brain. Why didn't he text? Why didn't he call? Did he think it was too forward to reach out the next day? Did he not actually want anything to do with me? Did he have a girlfriend? Did he find out that I had a boyfriend? Because, well, I had a boyfriend. Whom I loved. I hugged Dan's arm closer to my chest and closed my eyes, trying to make the thoughts go away.

I spent the next week trying to fight off these thoughts like a super ninja.

When I dreamt up the perfect man as a youth watching rom-coms in the 1990s, he was handsome, and not only was he smart and athletic, but he was also Ivy League smart and Division I football–scholarship athletic. He was over six feet tall and had a naturally tan complexion, with brown hair and brown eyes. He came from a big, close family; had a large, tightknit group of friends; had money in the bank; and had the ambition to quadruple that amount of money each year until retirement. He had the same favorite bands, artists, television shows, and movies as me, and had the same adoration for the beach, warm weather, and Starbucks coffee. He loved people, and people loved him. He was everyone's favorite person. He was perfect.

Dan, on the other hand, was handsome to me, was top-ten-in-his-high-school-class smart (which really means nothing, but he will appreciate my adding this), and was not coordinated enough for group sports but was athletic in terms of being able to run ten or more straight miles on a regular basis. He was just under six feet, with a complexion so pale he had to sit under the fucking pop-up tent at the beach to avoid getting sunburned. He had brown hair that had turned to no hair due to aging, and some facial hair to make up for it, and he had the most beautiful hazel eyes. He was an only child with a small, close group of friends. He had a decent job and more savings in the bank than I did. We loved the same television shows, which is a must for relationships today, because binge-watching is an essential part of being a functioning human being. He wasn't the biggest fan of the beach due to the whole pop-up-tent thing, and he preferred winter over summer. He was also an introvert and shy. He wasn't what I had deemed perfect years ago, but together, we fit.

But what if extraordinary love *did* exist, and I did not have it because I had never let myself hunt down my youth's idea of the dream man?

Dan and I were essentially the poster couple for opposites somehow attracting. I was a social butterfly who loved being around large groups of people and spending money I didn't have. He was a quiet bookworm who preferred small gatherings with close friends and saving money. Neither of us were each other's dream person, but somehow it just worked.

However, what if there was someone else out there who would work better for each of us? After all, I did not share Dan's love of history, nor did I get the obsession with watching Jeopardy every night at 7:30 p.m. My idea of a relaxing Saturday was to blast a Spotify playlist over some loud-ass speakers while cleaning, followed by going to Target for no reason, while his involved sitting at home reading a book in silence. Then there was the fact that he preferred vacationing in Maine, while I preferred Cape Cod. And then there was the fact that I preferred coffee from Starbucks, while he preferred coffee from Dunkin. And then there was the fact that he preferred budget hotels and restaurants, while I preferred fancy shit that, uh, I probably couldn't afford.

We were opposites, and it worked, but what if things could work better with someone else?

At the time, Dan and I had been talking about getting engaged soon. We had been together for six years, had lived together for three, and were ready to take the next step. Of course we were ready to take the next step. Everything was great, perfect, and as-it-should-be for a relationship like ours. But there was no reaching-for-the-stars, over-the-fence kind of stuff. No rom-com was being authored based on our love. No songs were being sung in public in order to win back my affection after a fight about some stupid shit.

> No songs were being sung in public in order to win back my affection after a fight about some stupid shit. Our relationship was great. But it wasn't *extraordinary*.

Our relationship was great. But it wasn't *extraordinary*. And I was terrified that good enough wouldn't be good enough forever. I was worried there was something more exceptional for each of us out there.

One week after these thoughts took over, I asked Dan to talk. It was time to take a break.

"I just don't know if this is right. For either of us," I told him.

"What are you talking about?" he said, rolling his eyes. He had heard this before, as most of our fights led to words like these, but no action had ever been taken.

"I'm serious this time. We've been fighting so much. And I feel like we really need to figure out if this is right."

"Of course it's right. We love each other."

"But what if love isn't enough? What if there's someone out there you wouldn't fight with as much that you'd be happier with? I just think we need to take some time apart to figure this out."

"I don't understand where this is coming from. Is there someone else?"

"No, that's insane," I responded, which was half true. No, there wasn't *actually* anyone else. Just the idea that PDM might actually have all the characteristics of the perfect man I'd dreamt up years ago—and that he might actually still reach out to me. Or, if not, that we might cross paths again so I could find this out.

"Just so you know, I love you. We're not perfect, but I love you."

"I love you too," I told him, fighting back tears. Why was I doing this?

As I watched him pick his duffel bag up and walk toward the bedroom to start packing, my heart sunk. I wanted to run after him, apologizing, and tell him to forget what I had just said. That this was a mistake. That I hadn't meant any of it. That I was just terribly confused about what love was supposed to look like. But I refrained.

He emerged from the bedroom with his backpack on and his duffel bag in his hands, not looking at me. As he opened the door to leave I started tearing up. A second later, he turned around and walked toward me, letting the door shut behind him. We hugged each other and cried.

"I understand why we need to do this. I just didn't want to admit it," he said, holding me tight.

"I know," I struggled to get out through tears. "Maybe this is a mistake. You don't need to go."

"But I do. You were right. This will only make us stronger."

I nodded. He kissed me on the forehead before saying goodbye and leaving. After the door shut, I broke down crying. What had I done?

I hadn't told friends what had been going on between us, so when I told them that Dan and I were on a break, they were a bit shocked. Not shocked that two humans so opposite from each other could decide to take some time apart, but shocked that we were having issues at all. I didn't even go into details about all of it or tell them about PDM. After all, it's a bit taboo to talk about insecurities and wandering eyes in long-term relationships, even after they end. You want people to root for your choice in a partner—not be in favor of you never speaking to a person you love ever again.

Because of this, I felt even more alone than I already was without Dan. The first couple of days, I texted and called him constantly, but later that week, we both agreed it wasn't going to work if we kept talking.

NOT BEING ABLE to talk to Dan was a challenge similar to the one I assume contestants go through on crazy survival game shows such as *Survivor* and *The Amazing Race*. I got teary eyed each morning that I didn't wake up next to him, each day at work I couldn't text him, and each night I didn't arrive home to his smiling face. It drove me insane not knowing what he was doing, but it drove me even more insane that I wasn't with him.

Before, it was PDM I couldn't seem to get off my mind, but now it was Dan. I began to wonder if PDM even existed. Like, was he just a façade? I didn't know anything about the man, other than what he did for work, where he'd gone to college, and how old he probably was based on when he'd graduated. I had become obsessed with finding out if this faux person could provide me with a better love than the one I had with Dan, but what was so wrong about that love? That he wasn't the perfect man I'd thought I would end up with when I was twelve years year old, lying on my bedroom floor listening to 'Nsync's "This I Promise You" and envisioning being in a real relationship one day?

The next weekend, I was out with friends. After two glasses of wine, they started telling me they didn't understand why I was so upset about not being with Dan.

"This was your idea," one told me.

"Dan is the only guy you've really ever been with. Now you can see what else is out there. There are plenty of dicks in the sea," my most adventurous friend said. I love living vicariously through her, but swimming through guys did not seem like the life for me. She added, "Plus I saw him on Tinder the other day."

Dan was on Tinder? I was shocked. I thought I was the only one curious about what else could be out there.

"You can do better than him anyway," another said.

This was the exact comment I had been trying to avoid by *not* telling my friends everything. What does this even mean, anyway? I know people think they're using the phrase "You can do better" as words of encouragement, but it is anything but that. First, it's demeaning. Basically, someone was looking at your relationship the whole time thinking you weren't living up to your potential. Thinking you had made a poor choice. Second, how do they know you can do better? Sure, you could find someone better looking. You could find someone who makes more money. You could find someone who gets along with your friends better. But what about finding someone you love more that loves you more? How could anyone be sure you can find that? And how could anyone assume you didn't have that in the first place?

Love is not about what things look like on the outside. It's about how you feel on the inside.

Later that night, other friends met up with us, bringing along other acquaintances too. At one point, I was sitting on a barstool, staring at my text history with Dan and fighting the urge to reach out, when one of the guys came up to me.

"Hey," he said.

"Hi," I said back, noticing my adventurous friend looking at us from afar. She was smiling while making the penis-in-the-vagina gesture with her hands. Our maturity level for being adults is sometimes ridiculously low.

I ended up talking with him for the majority of the night, partly out of loneliness and partly because I didn't want to get off the stool and lose my seat. After a while, he asked if I wanted to get out of there. I didn't know what to say. I mean, yes, I wanted to leave and go home. I had a frozen pizza waiting for me in the freezer that I had bought specifically for situations like this where I find myself drunk and hungrier than usual because I went out for dinner with friends and we "split appetizers," meaning I never really ate dinner. Maybe it would be nice to have some company to eat the pizza with. After all, the portion size was too much for one person. Maybe it would help me keep my mind off Dan. Maybe my friend was right about seeing what else was out there, and this was my chance.

"Sure," I told him, hopping off the barstool.

We left together and took an Uber back to my apartment.

Once there, we chatted and laughed about nonsense while making the frozen pizza, anxiously taking it out of the oven two minutes before it was done and eating it anyway. We brought the remaining slices over to the couch and turned on a movie. Then we awkwardly sat in silence, watching.

For thirty minutes, I internally panicked about everything. Why was this guy here? Why did I tell him to come? What would Dan do if he found out? Why wasn't I with Dan instead? Sitting on the couch and watching TV with Dan was one of my most favorite things to do. Doing so with this guy was not. It was awkward. Uncomfortable. Borderline soul crushing. I wanted him to leave, but I heard my friends' voices in my head. Seeing what else was out there was the real test. I had to know.

This guy had his arm stretched over my back, making for a very uncomfortable embrace. The kind where your back hurts from the arm pressing against it, but you've already mentioned it three times, and he's already tried moving his arm three times to no avail, so you just sit there and deal with it instead of bringing it up again. I debated breaking the silence multiple times, but maybe he was really into this movie, and we would speak again after. But it was late. I wanted to go to bed.

I decided I couldn't take it anymore and abruptly stood up, freeing my back from his arm.

"I'm going to bed," I told him.

"Okay," he looked at me.

"There's a blanket behind you." I pointed to the one ly-ing across the top of the couch before turning and walking toward the bedroom.

A few seconds later he stood up, walked after me, and put his hand on my behind. I turned back around, slightly surprised, and he kissed me.

I hadn't kissed another man in years. It felt weird, but human touch is intoxicating, so I went with it. I mean, sci-entifically, we are all animals. It only makes sense.

Before I knew it, we were in my bed, naked. He asked if I wanted to do "it," and I said yes, so we did.

That was it? I wondered to myself when it was over, as he rolled over to the other side of the bed. And not about the length of time the sex lasted—but about that being *it* for what else was out there. I just couldn't get over how awkward the entire scenario was. How uncomfortable it felt. Sure, this guy checked off more boxes on my perfect-man list than Dan did, and, sure, I had thought there might have been some sort of chemistry between us. But if there was, this would have felt normal. This would have felt right. And even if it did feel right to me, who's to say it felt right for him?

The next morning, we woke up and awkwardly laughed about the night before, each of us pretending we were too drunk to remember exactly what happened, because what else were we supposed to do in a situation like that? When he left, he didn't kiss me goodbye. Not on the mouth, or on the cheek. No hug, either. I figured he got what he was looking for. The good news is that I did too. The bad news is that I had to do all this to find it.

The next day, I made my friend go with me to CVS to buy Plan B. We had used protection, and I was on the pill, but for some reason taking Plan B made me feel better about the whole thing. In my mind, I felt like it erased the fact that this sex even happened. But that's not what Plan B is. I just convinced myself of this to feel better. But I didn't feel better.

Later that afternoon, I went to Bed Bath & Beyond to buy a new bedspread. A duvet, sheets, pillow covers, shams, the whole gang. I couldn't possibly sleep on my old bedspread anymore. It was stained with sins. I had to make the bed new again. Dan and I had talked about getting sheets with a better thread count anyway. I wished he could have been there with me to pick them out.

That night, I sat on my new duvet cover, scrolling through Dan's social media feeds that he posted to maybe twice a year, looking for any clue as to what he was doing. Was he talking to other people on Tinder? Was he sleeping with someone else? Was he happy?

Then, I started crying. Crying because I missed Dan. Crying because I wasn't with him, and I technically couldn't talk to him. Crying because this was all due to his not checking off the boxes on a perfect-man list I'd created when I was twelve years old. Crying because the guys who *did* check off most of the boxes were not in any way right for me. Crying because I had no one to talk to about this without being judged or being told "You can do better." Crying because I missed Dan, and I wanted him to come home.

I called him.

"Hello," he answered.

"I'm sorry," I cried into the phone. "I love you. Will you come home?"

Dan came home the next day. We hugged for approximately forty-six minutes as soon as he stepped foot inside our apartment.

ALL OF THE movies and television shows I had watched growing up that depicted love as an untouchable artifact were scams. Just as social media shows us the perfect parts of average people's lives, these movies and shows showed us the perfect parts of unrealistic lives, and so I felt cheated when reality didn't match that.

Love does not need to be extraordinary to be good enough. It does not need to stand out from other love. It does not need to be perfect all of the time. It does not need to make you shout from the rooftops, nor does it need to make you whistle while walking down a crowded street. It does not need to feel like you're at the World Series, and it does not

> Love does not need to be extraordinary. It does not need make you shout from the rooftops, nor does it need to make you whistle while walking down a crowded street.

mean you will be happy all of the fucking time. In fact, it is physically impossible to *always* be happy. You'd have to be a robot with zero emotions and hormones to do that.

When it comes to love, there is no perfect, and there is no mediocre. There is no right timing—there is just a time when it happens. After all, love is not a thing. It's a feeling between two people. A feeling you can't help because of science. Literally, because of science. They call it having chemistry for a reason.

Dan may not have been the man of my dreams, and I might not have been the woman of his dreams, but what we have together is better than anything we could have dreamt. We have that feeling. That connection.

If only I had known earlier that the dream is not to find a perfect person, but rather a perfect feeling. To find someone who feels like home. To find someone who makes you laugh. To find someone whose imperfections are worth it. Because at the end of the day, no one is perfect. Everyone is flawed. You just need to find someone it feels perfectly imperfect with.

When it comes to love, I'd rather have the ordinary than the extraordinary. I'd rather have the happy medium featuring the highs and lows, instead of just the highs. The lows make me appreciate the highs, and they make the mediocre in-betweens good enough. The highs are nice-to-have, but to be honest, they skew the numbers. That's why I love our ordinary love so much, and that's why I'll never doubt it ever again.

Why Perfect Couples Do Not Exist

PSA: Not everything is always as it seems.

I feel like I am always saying this to myself and other people. As humans, we constantly compare ourselves to others. The problem: we compare ourselves only to what we perceive, because we can never *really* know what something is like for someone else.

We compare our job situation to what we assume someone else's job situation is based on their title, without knowing their exact job responsibilities, their salary, or their true satisfaction with the whole thing.

We compare our financial situation to what we assume someone else's financial situation is based on the clothes they wear, the vacations they go on, and the area they live in, without knowing where that money is actually coming from and what their credit card balances look like.

We compare our friendships to other people's friendships based on pictures they post online, without knowing how often these people actually see each other and if everyone truly gets along.

And we compare our relationship to other people's relationships based on how that couple acts in public and what they post about each other online, without knowing what's really going on behind closed doors.

We create our own definitions for *average* based on these flawed assumptions and deem people who appear like they're doing better than we are above average and declare ourselves unimpressive because of it. But we must stop. Especially when it comes to relationships.

Thinking there are all these perfect couples out there can totally fuck with your love life. If you're in a relationship, it can make you second-guess it. Are you not going on enough dates? Are you not having enough sex? Are you not generally happy enough? And if you're not in a relationship, it can make you second-guess any prospective one. Is this person good-looking enough? Is this person impressive enough? Is this person making enough money?

You should be answering these questions based on your own thoughts, feelings, and beliefs, but your perception problems lead you to judge your own judgments. And then you spiral. You spiral hard.

Let's do a faux social media relationship perception spiral, shall we?

PRETEND YOU'RE SCROLLING through social media, and you see a parade of perfect-looking pictures, including but not limited to the following:

* **Pictures of a beautiful couple on a boat trip in Italy.** They are both wearing outfits that make it look like they are on an episode of *The Bachelor*. Not to mention, they both have perfect-looking faces and bodies good enough to be on *The Bachelor*. Why do these perfect-looking people also have just as perfect

financial situations so they can traverse across Italy? How does such a person become so perfect looking?

* **Pictures of a couple who just completed yet another marathon together.** Couples who run together stay together? But why? And how? How did two perfect marathoners find love?

* **Pictures of a baby celebrating three beautiful months of precious life.** She is swaddled in a blanket, lying on a white faux-fur rug, with minimalist décor of lush greenery all around. There is a loving note from the proud parents about what this baby likes and doesn't like, which, honestly, is impossible to really know, but whatever. How are these new parents already so perfect at their new jobs?

* **Pictures of a couple's beautiful new home in a town that has a great school system, with a note from the proud new owners, who "can't wait to start their next adventure."** They are standing in front of the home. They look like dots compared to the house. Why is the house so large? How could they afford that? How do they make all their money? Are they both equally as perfect at everything?

* **Pictures from a coworker's professional family photo shoot with his wife and two kids.** They are all

blonde and blue-eyed, wearing only the color white. They appear to be in a well-lit wooded area. You feel like these look like stock photos, and you wonder why they all look so perfect.

* **Pictures of an old acquaintance getting engaged.** They are on the beach, and she looks legitimately surprised. They both look happy. And also, very tan. Oh, they are on vacation. The ring is the size of my palm. Who is this formerly-average/newly-above-average person marrying?

* **Pictures of a family on vacation in the Bahamas with a couple of other families.** They are all friends. The parents, the kids, the grandparents. Or at least they all appear to be friends. They are all dressed nicely, enjoying cocktails, having a ball. Their trip seems perfect. Hell, their life seems perfect. How do perfect people find each other and come together to plan perfect trips like this?

After you binge-look into other peoples' romantic lives, you wonder how all these people are out there partaking in perfect relationships when your love life is so . . . average.

You rarely go on couples' vacations, and, when you do, they're fine. But "fine" to you is just not good enough when everyone else is projecting perfect. You want to go on more vacations with your partner, but you just don't have the money. (Or in some cases, the partner).

You don't have nearly enough money to afford a nice home in a nice area, and you're not sure if you'll ever be able to do that. You'll probably be able to purchase something good enough in a good-enough town soon, but "good enough" seems like a failure compared to everything you've been seeing other couples accomplish lately.

Neither of you are in amazing shape, but you're also not in horrible shape. You're just two mediocre people living mediocre lives. Even though you both love the way you each look, this still feels horrible to you based on how amazing all these other couples seem to look together.

And the families. Oh, the families. Perfect kids. Perfect financial situations. Perfect family friendships. Perfect vacations. Perfect outfits.

Meanwhile, you're on the couch, scrolling through your phone, comparing your own love life to the spectacle of bullshit that is social media.

This has got to stop.

Just because a couple posts pictures of big achievement milestones, writes extraordinary love notes about each other, and showcases their seemingly perfect, everyday lives to the world online does not mean they are perfect. After all, what *is* perfect? Does perfect even exist? Is perfect just a hoax?

Kind of, yes. Especially when you are describing someone else's life or certain situations as such.

NOW, LET'S TAKE a look at those same posts on social media but with a different eye. This time, we're going to focus on *all* hints of bullshit that give away that these posts might not really be so perfect after all:

* **Pictures of a beautiful couple on a boat trip in Italy.** Did this couple actually have the money for that trip, or did they rack up a fuck ton of credit card debt by taking it? If they did have the funds, were they even theirs to begin with? And what about the outfits? How do they have all that money for the clothes and the vacations—and the personal training? Clearly these people do not fuck around when it comes to their toned and muscular bodies, but where do they find the time? Are they just always working and exercising? Do they ever see each other? I guess they got to go on this trip. But were they as happy as they looked in the photos they posted the entire trip, or did they fight about random shit like whether to walk or take a cab to dinner? Because if they didn't fight on vacation, the conclusion here is that these people are actually robots.

* **Pictures of a couple who just completed yet another marathon together.** I'm not going to get into this one. Can someone please tell marathoners it's okay to be unimpressive? Thanks.

* **Pictures of a baby celebrating three beautiful months of precious life.** Is the baby always this adorable and quiet? Are the parents not in the picture because they didn't want anyone to see the bags under their eyes? Are they currently suffering from a severe lack of sleep as a result of a screaming baby? Have they stopped having sex? Do they cry sometimes from the stress? God bless greenery for hiding all of this, right?

* **Pictures of a couple's beautiful new home in a town that has a great school system, with a note from the proud new owners, who "can't wait to start their next adventure."** First of all, fuck your new adventure, because I am not buying this. How the fuck did these two people afford that house? Trust fund? Drug money? Please advise. If the money *is* from work, do these people ever see each other? Do they ever have sex? Will they ever be in that house together? Are they really even all that happy? Sure, they have a nice house, but happiness is not an object.

* **Pictures from a coworker's professional family photo shoot with his wife and two kids.** Does this family always appear this perfect, or is this just staged and edited? Are the kids a handful? Do they whine all the time? Is the couple still in love? Are their busy lives causing them to grow apart? Do they even still sleep in the same bed?

* **Pictures of an old acquaintance getting engaged.**
  Was this new engagement a surprise, or was it brought
  on by an ultimatum to propose by a certain time or
  else? I mean, honestly. What was the real kick in the
  ass that got this decision going?

* **Pictures of a family on vacation in the Bahamas
  with a couple other families.** Multiple families going
  on vacation together sounds like a shit show. Why do
  it? Also, who is cheating on whom, and when is it
  going to become public?

Notice how those were extremely different glances into
the same exact worlds? It's true—we really all see what we
want to see. We make shit up in our heads, tell ourselves lies,
and base our own feelings of self-worth off of that.

But this is not okay to do. Whether we're assuming everything is perfect or searching for hints of flaws, we need
to stop. We must strive for the happy medium of judging,
which is accepting things for what they are. We need to focus on our own lives and feelings and ignore the rest.

It doesn't matter how a couple looks, acts, or promotes
themselves. Pictures and appearances do not tell the story of
a relationship. This is why we're always so surprised when
celebrities, people who recently got married, and couples
who post about their love for one another online break up.
Everything seemed perfect between them, but that's because
we were only seeing small glimpses into their lives. They

showcased the great, hid the bad, and ignored the mediocre. We may have thought we were less exceptional because of it, but in reality they had average issues—just like us.

Here's the thing. When it comes to love, it is never about what something looks like. It's always about what something feels like. I can tell you right now, the only people who can know whether or not something is perfect are the two people in the relationship. It doesn't matter what they post online. It doesn't matter if they look good together in pictures. It doesn't matter if they look like they are in love while shopping for groceries on Sunday afternoon. What matters is that they love each other.

So, do perfect couples exist? I guess that's up for debate. Technically, nothing is perfect. Everything has flaws. But if something feels perfect to you, despite all its defects, then call it what you want. Just stop judging other people or making assumptions based on a surface representation. You can never know what's really going on when it comes to something you're not part of.

Quiz: Is Your Partner Average or Just an Asshole?

__ Talks about themselves—a lot: *Average*
__ Talks about themselves all the time, never asking about you: *Asshole*

__ Does not respond to your text messages when they are in a meeting at work: *Average*

__ Gets mad at you for not responding to text messages when you're in a meeting at work: *Asshole*

__ Asks if it would be okay to cancel plans at the last minute because something came up with old friends: *Average*

__ Cancels plans with you at the last minute to hang out with new friends: *Asshole*

__ Leaves dirty dishes out overnight: *Average*

__ Leaves dirty dishes out every night even though you ask for them to be put away: *Asshole, with a slight hint of average*

__ Says no to going on vacation, because they want to save more money first: *Average*

__ Says no to going on vacation because they have no interest in going where you want to go: *Asshole*

__ Gets jealous when others show interest in you: *Average*

__ Starts a fight when others show interest in you: *Asshole*

__ Complains about their job but doesn't get a new one: *Average*

__ Does not have a career and has zero interest in finding one: *Asshole*

__ Likes to know when you make plans with other people: *Average*

__ Needs to know when you make plans with other people: *Asshole*

__ Compliments you on your looks: *Average*

__ Tells you how you should look: *Asshole*

__ Asks you for help with their problems: *Average*

__ Blames you for their problems: *Asshole*

__ Asks you to do things: *Average*

__ Tells you what to do: *Asshole*

__ Says and shows how sorry they are when they fuck up: *Average*

__ Only says how sorry they are when they fuck up: *Asshole*

The 10 Commandments of Love for Us Commoners

1. Thou shall not compare thy average relationship to anyone else's.

"Why don't we go out to dinner as much as [insert other couple here]?"

"Every other couple goes on vacations and trips all the time. Why don't we?"

"You never post about me on social media like other people do. Do you not love me?"

Long story short: no two relationships are the same. There is no average when it comes to relationships as a whole. There is just the average that you define yourself in your own relationship. This is because every couple is different. Every type of love is different. Your relationship isn't full of below-average love just because you're not shouting about it from the rooftops on social media. Your relationship isn't boring just because you prefer to stay in instead of going out, or because you prefer to save money instead of constantly spending it on vacations. If your relationship isn't making you happy, it's not because of other people's relationships—it's because something is causing you to be unhappy. Stop focusing on other people and figure out what that thing is yourself. In the end, all that matters is that you are happy.

2. Thou shall understand that no matter what, if someone wants to be with you, they'll find the happy medium to do so.

I feel like rom-coms have destroyed us—both for adding the word *rom-com* to our vocabulary and for being unrealistic. We were made to believe in fairy tales and in Harry and Sally's relationship, which I am a fan of, but also, if they really wanted to be together, why didn't they just admit it earlier?

Life is not a movie script or a romantic novel. It's just a bunch of average humans running around with the animal instinct to mate with people they are attracted to. No games. Just straight up sex with the potential for love making, and if love is made (with or without sex), humans act on that right away, usually acting like idiots because love does weird-ass things to people. That being said, if someone wants to be with you, they'll want to talk to you and hang out with you and *be* with you. No, things do not have to be perfect for an ordinary couple. They just have to be good enough. And what's meant to be good enough will always find a way. There's no need for you to sit around waiting for a text back to figure that out.

3. Thou shall listen to thy "meh" gut feelings.

Things don't need to be great all the time in an average person's world, but if something is telling you things are not good enough anymore, it's probably time to move on. Your feelings don't lie. If something doesn't feel right, it's probably not right. For example, if you think they might be cheating, there's a chance they could be cheating (but there's also a chance they might NOT be cheating; it's like I always say—peruse before you accuse; actually I've never said that before, but I think I'm going to now?). If you think you might not feel the same way anymore, you've probably lost that feeling. Basically, you shan't ignore your feelings. You deserve good enough. Don't forget that.

4. Thou shall give good-enough connections a chance.

If you feel a connection with someone, it is an ordinary thing to want to explore whether or not that feeling is love. This is, after all, how dating works. Or it's how dating *used* to work before it became judging people based on one's looks and interests on an app. You don't get to see if you have that connection until after you go through the trouble of communicating via a smartphone and planning to meet in person. This whole ordeal is honestly ridiculous because it takes a few seconds in person to know if you have that initial chemistry. First dates now should really just be "let's meet in front of the bar, chat for two minutes, and then decide if we want to continue with a real date." The date still might suck, but you'd probably be able to weed out a good portion of people. Regardless of how you meet someone, if you feel any hint of a connection with them, pursue it. It doesn't matter if they seem ordinary and unimpressive to you—the connection is what is most important here. Plus, to be human is to be ordinary, and to be ordinary is to be unimpressive. Let us not forget this.

5. Thou shall talk about all the ordinary things thou wants in life with thy partner because it's always important to make sure your mediocre worlds mesh.

Do you want to get married? Do you want to travel? What is your stance on kids? What is your vision of a "dream home?" Where do you want to live? How do you value money? It is never too early to discuss important, average life shit like this in a relationship. Why spend part of your life with someone to later find out their idea of ordinary is completely different from yours? You can either figure out early on if you can compromise on your differing wants, OR you can avoid bringing up the hard topics until much later and hope your significant other will eventually be on the same page as you, risking going through a hard-as-fuck breakup if that isn't the case. Not to mention, during the time you spent with them, you could have been out there enjoying life independently, maybe meeting someone who shares your values and dreams, or who would at least be a happy medium.

6. *Thou shall leave their below-average ass if they are unsure about their future with you.*

If they won't commit, you must quit. But seriously, stop thinking this is going to happen. It's not going to happen. And even if it does eventually happen, do you really want to end up with someone who, for a period of time, was all, "Yeah, I don't know if I want to be with you forever yet. Can you just, like, hang tight while I decide?" I mean, WHAT? No, you cannot hang tight and delay your potential future while waiting for someone else to decide if you will be part of their potential future. You need to get out there and move on while they decide. And if they end up deciding their future is you, and your future still has an available slot for them, well then there you go—now you can be together. But don't fucking sit around and wait. That's pathetic. You're not pathetic.

7. Thou shall accept when things are no longer sufficient.

Relationships can be hard, yes. They take work. But if you keep putting in work, and things are rarely ever good enough, there comes a time when you need to stop and question if this is meant to work at all. Just because something seems perfect on paper doesn't mean it's right. Just because things are good most of the time doesn't mean you should ignore the times that are bad. You can't force yourself or someone else to want and like certain things. You can't force someone to change. You can't force happiness, and you certainly can't force love. What you can do is embrace your own average life and let go of the things in it that are below average.

8. Thou shall repeat after me: sometimes love isn't [good] enough.

And that's okay. Yes, I am telling you firsthand that although you may love the fuck out of each other, that doesn't mean your relationship will defy all odds and work out no matter what. It's exactly what I said above: sometimes love isn't enough. Maybe you don't want to give up the chance to have kids to be with the person you love, who doesn't want kids. Maybe you fight about literally everything, and you don't want to be in a toxic relationship anymore. Maybe your worlds just don't mesh together well, and they never will. Whatever the case, it's okay. We humans were not put on this earth as characters in a video game where the object is to find the one person out there for us. There is not only one person out there for each of us, so it's okay if something doesn't work out. If you want to, you can find love again.

9. Thou shall not shut thyself off from average love in hopes of finding unbelievable, out-of-this-world love.

Average love is love, too. Just like it's okay for you to be average, it's okay for your love life to be average too. You're not doing anything wrong because you're not having an extraordinary amount of sex. You're not doing anything wrong because you don't walk down the street hand-in-hand. You're not doing anything wrong because the love isn't as exciting as it was when you first met. This is just life, people. Know the difference between good enough and not enough, because love that is good enough is often one of the greatest loves of all. Too much passion can lead you down a fiery road, and not in a good way.

10. Thou shall never base a decision in thy love life on a timeline thou made up years ago, and instead shall embrace the mediocre spontaneity of life and love itself.

FUCK. YOUR. TIMELINE. Not only are you allowed to live life at your own speed, but you also can't control when shit happens. Don't want to get married or have kids? That's fine. Want to get married, but not yet? Don't. But if you meet someone who changes your mind about that, don't be hesitant just because the timeline says it's not time for that yet. Worried about meeting someone in time to have kids before it's too late? Put yourself out there and see if you can find that connection. But also explore other options, and don't think you've failed because you haven't found love. Love is special, right? Well, wouldn't it be pretty un-special if everyone who wanted to was able to find love at the same time? Yes.

So many people have these timelines. "Get engaged at twenty-six, get married at twenty-seven, have first kid before turning thirty." I mean, that's what I always told myself. But then I turned twenty-six, and I was in no rush to be married. And then I turned thirty, and I was in no way ready to have a child (although if it had happened, I was at a point where I would be okay figuring out how to roll with it, negative money in the bank and all). It was then I realized this was all okay. Why was I in such a rush? What was I trying to prove? People get married at all ages, some multiple times, some not at all, and although age matters when it comes to getting pregnant for women, there are so many options now for doing that later in life if you want to.

In the end, you need to do shit because you want to do it when you want to do it, and you need to roll with life's punches when it hits you with unplanned events. There's nothing below average about taking life at your own speed. What is below average is chasing after things just because you think you're supposed to have them. But you're not special. You're average. And wouldn't you rather live the average life that you're meant to live than chase after a special life that will never feel right? I'd take the good-enough life any day.

THE

**I GIVE ZERO FUCKS ABOUT
WHAT I SEE ONLINE!**

AWARD

IS EVERYONE MORE IMPRESSIVE THAN YOU ON SOCIAL MEDIA?

. . . and other thoughts about overachievers' Pinterest-perfect lives

Why You Need to Stop Giving a Fuck About What People Think of Your Average Life

Social media anxiety. Noun. A feeling of unease about being ordinary compared to everyone else online.

For years, my life consisted of waking up, checking my social feeds, going to school or work, and then checking my social feeds. My online presence was more important to me than my presence in real life. I saw it as a chance to get people to like me—people who might think I was annoying in real life, or maybe who would just never take the time to get to know me. Social media was my shot at being noticed, at getting people to think my life was active and interesting, to discover I was deep and meaningful.

The sad part about this is that even as the social media game has changed over the years, from AOL to MySpace to Facebook to Instagram to Whathaveyou, the desire to make oneself appear impressive online has not. In fact, it's only gotten more intense, and the competition has gotten more accomplished. We've raised the bar for what ordinary actually is, even though most of what we see is fake (an edited image), unrealistic (one of two hundred images taken of the same scene, the others of which never see the light of day because they aren't great), or unattainable (all those wealthy bloggers out there you see traveling the world).

For way too long, we've been letting social media get the best of us, and guess what? We have to stop. Let's dive into why.

—

I'VE ALWAYS CRAFTED my online profiles in a way that I hoped made me seem less average than I actually was. AOL profiles used to ask for your marital status, and although I was perpetually single, I always came up with a way to make it look like my romantic life was thriving. Whether I was throwing in the "single and ready to mingle" line or covering the answer with many hearts (<3), I couldn't let people know how bland my love life was.

Then there was the profile decor. Decorating my online profiles back in the day clearly foreshadowed how into decorating my home I would later become. The font colors, background colors, and font styles were all so important to me because they helped my profile stand out from everyone else's. I took pride in the fact that I did not use the most basic and average font of all, Comic Sans, which I strongly believe is the equivalent to the "Live, Laugh, Love" wall art you can buy at your nearest HomeGoods. My profiles (and later, my living room) were modern and chic, reflecting the life of someone talented and extraordinary—not unimpressive and extra ordinary. Or at least that's what I wanted people to perceive.

In addition to how it looked, I also carefully crafted the text that went inside my profiles. The song lyrics I posted were an attempt to get people to think I was cool based on the music I was listening to. The quotes I posted were an attempt to make people think I had an interesting and drama-filled life, when in fact things were pretty drama free on my end. The inside jokes I posted were an attempt to make it seem like I had an exciting social life, when really it was pretty ordinary.

I posted more for other people than for myself, all so I could impress them by hiding my extremely average life. But what was so wrong with my extremely average life?

Well, compared to what everyone else was posting online, it seemed pretty shitty, and I was embarrassed by it. My life wasn't supposed to be suboptimal. It was supposed to be glitz and glamour. So I used social media to pretend that it was by posting fabulous photos and happy life updates—all the fucking time. Until I realized that was no longer "cool." (Was it ever? I'm not sure.)

When I first started using Instagram, my younger brother asked me why I was posting so much.

"Isn't that what you're supposed to do?" I responded. My experience since getting my first screen name in the 1990s had been "overshare or don't share at all," so why would have I thought otherwise?

"No, it's embarrassing. You're only supposed to post once a day," he informed me.

Supposed to post once a day. I'm only *supposed* to post one picture a day. *Who is making up these rules?* I wondered. "I don't need to follow fake social media rules made up by kids," I laughed on the outside while thoughts started spinning around inside my head. I was posting too much. I had to stop!

This revelation led to many stressful hours spent debating what photo to post online—and when to post it. No exaggeration. A few days after I returned home from a trip to Greece, Chrissy Teigen savagely tweeted about how people need to stop posting pictures from vacation after they arrive home. While on vacation, I had made sure not to post more than one photo a day because of the unwritten rule I'd learned from my brother, so when I got home I had many pictures left to share. This left me panicking about whether I could still post my vacation pictures even though I was no longer on vacation.

I used to be that person on social media who overshared. My away message would tell you when I was showering, and my Facebook status would tell you that I was at the library then cheerleading practice then watching *True Blood*. I didn't have to worry about posting the *right* stuff. I just shared everything that popped into my head—and more.

When oversharing became uncool, I started to only post things that I believed made my profile look truly extraordinary, and if I didn't get a certain amount of likes on the post in a certain number of minutes, I would delete it. I didn't use to be like that. In fact, if you look at my activity on social media from ten years ago, I recklessly posted on social media—no likes necessary. Suddenly, though, it became all about posting the right stuff at the right time so I could get the most likes, or, in other words, so I could get the most validation that I was not ordinary—I was great. I was successful. I was impressive. And it wasn't just me who was so consumed by needing validation. Suddenly everyone was.

Things were so much easier when we didn't care. Why did we have to start caring? We destroyed ourselves, I'm telling you.

Comparing Yourself to Others Online Will Ruin You

Pictures are not the only things I've posted online in hopes of impressing people. My job title is another thing that has caused me social media anxiety. On LinkedIn, this is how we are defined. Although job titles are just words and can have different meanings at different companies, it can hurt to see your peers working at great companies in what seem to be higher positions than you. It can make you feel inadequate and mediocre.

For too long, I obsessed over all of these things. I was more focused on getting a job title that would impress others on social media than on getting a job I would actually enjoy. I defined my self-worth by how many likes my pictures and status updates got. I looked at what everyone else was posting on social media and beat myself up over the fact my life didn't seem as good.

"I am SO excited to announce that I accepted an offer for my dream job today. Life really does work in mysterious ways," an old classmate would write on Instagram.

"It's official—I'm moving to New York City next month!" an old coworker would tweet.

"Rome->Florence->Venice->Paris->London," a peer would title an album on Facebook to show off their recent travels.

"James started a new job as a Director at [Insert Dream Company Here]," LinkedIn would inform me.

And there I was—23 years old, sitting in bed, my Mac-Book on my lap, scrolling through my social media news-feeds and peering into everyone else's lives instead of living mine.

Envious of how fabulous my peers' lives seemed, I felt a constant need to spice mine up. Whether this meant mov-ing to a nicer area, living in a bigger home, carrying around a more expensive bag, or vacationing more often, I had to make myself appear less mediocre than I felt.

This is how my social-media-anxiety-induced debt grew. Vacations, expensive wine, organic groceries, boutique fit-ness classes, "affordable" designer handbags, trendy clothes, every pair of sandals Target sold from 2011 to 2016, home décor, fucking THROW PILLOWS—if it would make me ap-pear more exceptional than I was, I bought it.

On the outside, I was trying to project perfect. But on the inside, I was crumbling.

"Every other couple goes on vacation. Why don't we?" I would say to Dan from the couch while scrolling through Facebook. "This is insane. We never do anything fun to-gether. We don't even go on dates. Why are we together?"

"Stop comparing us to other couples," he would respond.

But I couldn't let it go. Pictures of happy couples in Hawaii, the Bahamas, Italy, and Paris filled my Facebook and Instagram feeds. They made me question my relationship.

Why can't we afford trips like all these other couples? What are we doing wrong? We barely even go on dates. Shouldn't we be going on more dates? Do we not spend enough money on each other? Does this mean he doesn't love me? Does this mean I don't love him? Does he not make enough money to make me happy? Do I not make enough money to make me happy? Will either of us *ever* make enough money?

One time after I had accepted a new job offer for more money, I convinced him to go on a trip to Miami with me to celebrate. My thinking was that we could put it on a credit card and pay it back with the extra money I'd start making upon our return. We got a room at a great hotel for an amazing price and figured we'd bring a couple hundred dollars for spending money. We thought we would only owe about $600 for the whole trip. However, within thirty minutes of getting there, we were presented with a receipt for two $25 margaritas. Soon after that, we were greeted with a parade of receipts for $30 salads, $75 steaks, and $100 wine bottles. I'm pretty sure he is still mad about the surprise cost of this vacation.

Did I ever tell anyone about the debt, anxiety, and arguments this one trip caused us after we got home? No way. Instead, I posted pictures of us smiling in front of the camera. I posted pictures of the ocean view from our room's balcony. I posted pictures of me in head-to-toe coordinated outfits purchased two weeks before the trip.

The image projected to others on social media was that I was thriving and my love life was solid. The reality was that I was racking up unnecessary credit card debt, and it was taking a toll on my relationship.

The desire to make my life appear more exciting ramped up after this. I wanted people to come to my Instagram page and see success. Carefully coordinated, expensive, trendy outfits. Trips to new places. A serious love life. An envious family life. Friends! So many friends! As I tried harder to keep up appearances, my peers seemed to be doing the same, but I never thought of it that way. I just assumed they were all better off than me and that I was the only one pretending. In fact, I still do it now.

Looking at my peers on social media, I get jealous when I see people hanging out with friends all the time. Do you know how insane that is? I don't see my friends as much anymore, but I'm sure people on social media think I see them all the time based on the pictures I post of us. Sure, we used to see each other every weekend, but now we get together once every month or two.

I get jealous when I see someone going to yet another country on their bucket list, when I'm probably going to be paying back the one trip I took to Greece for years to come. I mean, my Instagram posts from Santorini might be picture perfect—but that doesn't mean my life is.

I get jealous when I see a perfect-looking couple on Facebook who seem to go out to dinner all the time and hang out with couples who all seem to love each other—even though someone who sees any picture of me and my husband would assume that about us too, because what other story does a picture of smiling people tell?

I even get jealous when I see people's pictures of healthy, homemade dinners, especially when I haven't cooked in three weeks and keep getting takeout—but why would anyone know that, when I used to broadcast my gourmet Weight Watchers meal creations on Instagram with their own fucking hashtag—#adultinginthekitchen. Let me tell you the story behind this hashtag. I cooked, like, eight meals in a year and decided I could be the next Martha Stewart. Alas, I was not. I got lazy . . . and jealous of everyone else cooking on social media . . . and then I started to feel inadequate. But why?

It's fucking bullshit that I feel this way. It's fucking bullshit that anyone feels this way. I'm not the only person who has trouble coordinating dates and times to see friends. I'm not the only person putting trips on credit cards. And I'm certainly not the only one who isn't always 100 percent happy with their love life. All of this is average and ordinary. For some reason, though, we try to hide the fact that we're normal, and it hurts us.

If We All Stopped Projecting Perfection, We'd Be Happy with Being Average

The truth is, we all often feel average—and a good chunk of us work hard at making ourselves and our lives appear less average on social media. We then go on living a lie while feeling average, because we forget that the people we are comparing ourselves to are likely living lies too.

Do you *really* think the travel blogger you follow is always traveling and never spends a weekend cleaning and never misses their friends and family? Do you *really* think the fashion blogger you love isn't in some sort of credit card debt from shopping? Do you *really* think that *everyone* you know is truly happy in his or her relationship? Do you *really* think that everyone who says they're making a lot of money is really making a lot of money?

We say that social media's impact on society is getting worse. We worry about kids growing up with all of these platforms, like we never dealt with this shit before. But the problem isn't social media. It's that social media is a platform for *our* lies.

I've been crafting exactly how I want other people to perceive me online since I got my first screen name when I was in third grade. I've been worried about what other people think of me since I overheard girls in my dance class call me annoying behind my back when I was nine. I've been comparing my body to other girls' bodies since I first picked up a magazine.

What we all need to realize is that, just like we compare our bodies to bodies in magazines that have been retouched, we're comparing our lives to lives that have been retouched. People airbrush their relationships and Photoshop their happiness. They edit their own stories through text and imagery and never offer others the opportunity to watch the deleted scenes. They share what they want—and we, the followers, accept their story as fact, as who this person really is.

I always wonder what would happen if I stopped giving a fuck. If I said, "Fuck it, I don't care if people see me repeating the same outfits over and over again. I don't care what people will think if I take pictures of my subpar body in a bikini at the beach. I don't care that my salary is one-third the salary most of my friends are making. I don't care that I don't have enough money saved to buy a nice house like so many of my peers who keep announcing their investments on Facebook."

The thing is—no one gives a fuck about our finances, our bodies, or our outfits—except ourselves. No one is deeming us a more successful human for having a designer bag or being able to travel to Europe. If only we had learned from our AIM activity back in the day. No one gave a fuck about the song lyrics in our away messages or all of the friends' initials we filled our profiles with. None of our cool screen names attracted new friends, and none of the quotes we put in our profiles to pretend we had a boyfriend helped us to get an actual boyfriend (oh, that was just me? Never mind).

We attract friends in real life. We develop interests in real life. We make careers in real life. We are happy in real life— and sometimes we are sad in real life, and that's fine. We are not robots. We have emotions.

All I'm asking is that we do better when it comes to toying with each other's emotions. We can brag. We can share adventures. We can post selfies. But let's stop lying. Let's stop exaggerating. Let's stop hiding the mediocre and only showcasing the extraordinary. And let's remember: we never truly know what's going on in someone's real life—never mind what's going on in a picture or status update. It's all perception. If we start being more realistic about things, perhaps we'll start separating the lies from the truth, and we'll start perceiving things differently. Then maybe, just maybe, we'll be able to embrace our own ordinary, as well as everyone else's.

How Much Social Media Anxiety Has the Internet Given You over the Years?

A CHECK YO AVERAGE SELF LIST

Give yourself one point for every checkmark.

__ You have envied someone else's better-than-average-looking life online.

__ You have questioned whether you have a good-enough amount of friends after seeing how many friends other people have.

__ You have been enraged that someone posted an unexceptional photo of you online.

__ You have driven yourself insane trying to choose which better-than-average pictures to post on social media and which less-than-average photos to hide.

__ You have deleted a photo or a post on social media because it didn't get an above-average number of likes.

__ You have changed your profile picture more than two times within a month in hopes of appearing more impressive.

__ You have spent over five minutes editing a picture of yourself to make it look better than ordinary.

__ You have thought people didn't like you because your posts on social media were receiving meh interactions.

__ You have gotten upset because "not enough" people wished you happy birthday online.

__ You have gotten nervous about what to say to someone when responding to or sending a message online in fear of sounding just okay.

__ You have ignored a message online because you thought it would make you look desperate if you responded right away (or because you were nervous about what to say).

__ You have forgotten to respond to someone's message online—and it still haunts your average dreams.

__ You don't understand why you can't flag online messages like you can flag emails to respond to them later.

__ You have posted something online in an attempt to make it look like your romantic life is more exciting than it actually is.

__ You have posted something online in an attempt to make it look like your family is doing better than they actually are.

__ You have posted something online in an attempt to make it look like your social life is more exceptional than it actually is.

__ You have posted something online in an attempt to make it look like your financial status is more impressive than it actually is.

__ You have wished your life was more impressive so you'd have more to post online.

__ You have looked at an old significant other's social media profile multiple times to see how you compare.

__ You have looked at your significant other's exes' social media profiles multiple times to see how you compare.

__ You have looked at an old significant other's exes' or new flame's social media profiles multiple times to see how you compare.

__ You have gotten nervous thinking WHAT IF people could possibly see how many times you view their profile.

__ You have refused to look through certain photo albums or galleries on social media because you were afraid you would accidentally "like" something.

__ You refuse to give people your phone to look at something on one of your social media accounts in fear they'll accidently like something, leaving you to look like a subpar social media user.

__ You have given someone your phone to look at something on one of your social media accounts, panicked as they scrolled through it, and yelled at them to give you back the phone after a few seconds.

__ You have checked your activity logs on social media to see if you've been caught in the less-than-average act of accidentally liking a post from a person you shouldn't have been stalking.

__ You have been upset about a major unimpressive life change because everyone on social media would have to find out.

__ You have complained on Twitter about Instagram or Facebook being down.

__ You have sat there and thought *What am I supposed to do now?* after your phone has died and you can't check social media.

__ You have nearly cried after the internet has gone out, because you can't go on social media.

__ You hate the internet because it gave you social media.

__ You love the internet because it gave you social media.

0: None, but You Probably Lied

Do you even use the internet? No? Are you the ghost of pre-internets past? You must be. Get out of here.

1–5: A Tiny Bit

Assuming you did not lie while going through the checklist, you're doing fine. It's normal to sometimes get attached to the things you use every day (i.e., the internet), and it's normal to sometimes compare yourself to others. As long as you don't go overboard and obsess and panic over such things, you're going to be okay. Keep doing you.

5–15: A Decent Amount

Sometimes you let the internet get the best of you, but the good news? Not all the time. You might have cared more about things on the internet when you were younger, and now might sometimes question your own life after looking into another person's life online, but you're self-aware. You know what you're doing, and you stop yourself before you go completely overboard. Just keeping reminding yourself, "Not everything is real online; it's just the internet," and you'll be fine.

15–25: I Mean, A Lot

Alright. You *might* be on the brink of a meltdown brought on by a little something called internet addiction, but you aren't there quite yet. Perhaps that's because you realized your bad habits and stopped them already, or perhaps it's because you stop yourself from caring too much because part of you *knows* that things in real life are not always as they seem online. However, part of you also tends to think WHAT IF all these things are real? What if people don't like you? What if your relationship is a sham? What if you're doing worse in life than all your peers are? STOP THINKING THIS STUFF. Get offline, put your phone away, go outside, and smell the roses. If there are no roses, smell the air. This is going to be way more refreshing than doing literally anything on the above checklist; you're welcome, bye.

25+: A Shit Ton

Hello, my name is Sam, and I am going to lead you in an intervention today: you need to disconnect yourself from technology ASAP. Yes, that's right. Hide your computer, hide your phone, and unplug Netflix. You need a mother-fucking break. Clearly the internet has been riding your ass since you were given access to its realm, and clearly you need some time away to become your own person again sans internet (if you were even born before the internet, that is). Not everything online is real. Not everyone online is watching you.

Is everyone on social media having more fun than you?

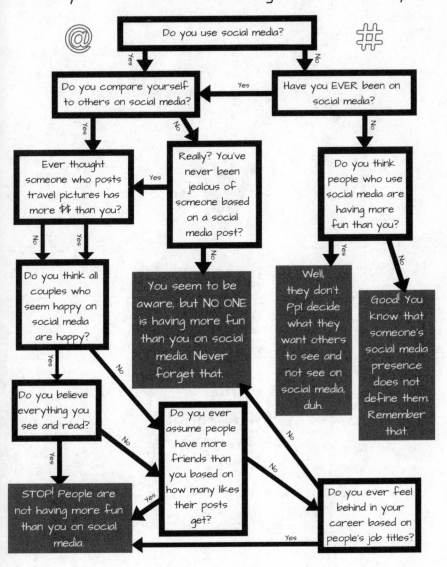

THE
I DID A THING!
AWARD

WHY DOES IT FEEL LIKE WE'VE ACCOMPLISHED NOTHING WHEN WE HAVE?

... and other thoughts about life on the hump of the bell curve

Letter to My Younger, Average Self About Embracing the Happy Medium

Dear nine-year-old Sam,

Hi. It's me. Grown-up you. Things up on this hill are good, thanks for asking. I should let you know, though, we don't have a cat. They don't allow them in the building we live in, which sucks, but we're hoping to get one when we move. I hope you take pride in knowing that we are still cat people. Crazy, right? Even though so much has changed, we pretty much stayed the same. We even have the same dream: to become a cat, which we proudly wrote as our desired career in our kindergarten yearbook. What's funny is how at a young age we knew this was a figurative dream that could never actually happen. We just want to sleep all day, manipulate people into feeding us, and make loud noises until we get what we want. All of this was and still is perfectly acceptable.

See—you're funny. Don't let your mediocrity make you think you're unimpressive. You're just average, meaning you're normal. To the girls you heard calling you annoying from the other room before dance class a few weeks ago, fuck them (sorry for the language, but, to be honest, that's nothing we haven't already heard; I mean, our first sentence was "I have to take a leak," so we were born with a literal potty mouth). Yes, you're annoying. Yes, you talk too much. But those two things are normal. And they are going to help you go places later in life. Don't hide your personality in fear of people not liking you. Don't try to be someone you're not. Just be your average self, and happiness will follow.

Continue embracing your ordinary interests, too. Keep talking about stuff you like. Keep watching stuff that makes you laugh. Keep playing the Spice Girls at recess. Keep listening to Biggie Smalls and Elton John (it's making you well rounded). Oh, and be nicer to your dad. He sat through Spice Girls, 'Nsync, and Backstreet Boys concerts for you. Show some respect.

So, keep writing in that little flower-covered diary, and keep jotting down stories in your black composition notebooks. You might think your life is too unexceptional to write about it for the world, but keep doing it for yourself, and you'll realize that you're wrong. You're on to something, you relatable soul, you. You just don't know it yet.

And please, as you grow older, never doubt the fact that you are a great human. You are smart, you are beautiful, you have talents, and you have a good gut—no, I'm not talking about your belly, I'm talking about your instincts. You may not be the Best and Most Impressive when it comes to all kinds of crap, but when you find your happy medium, you'll know you're in the beautiful place you are meant to be.

xoxo,

Sam

10 Average Accomplishments Average People Can Be Supremely Proud Of

1. Getting yourself an education.

I guess I owe this one to my parents, especially my mom, who attempted to wake me up for school approximately seventeen times each morning after I snoozed through my alarms before I finally got up. If it weren't for her doing this, I most definitely would have slept through the entirety of school.

Screw getting a degree; managing to move my lazy ass off of my bed each morning was the real accomplishment.

If you were able to wake up in the morning and get your ass out of bed for school, too, you should be proud . Even if it was easy for you to do the whole morning thing, you should be proud of yourself for going to school. It doesn't matter if you graduated with honors or took AP classes. It doesn't matter what activities you were part of or what college you went to. Hell, it doesn't even matter if you went to college. There's no need to feel unimpressive at this task just because you got an ordinary education. You went to school. You learned some shit. And now, thanks to that, you are an educated person. That is a cause for applause.

2. Having a job that chose you out of a bunch of other applicants.

"Why me?" is a question I find myself asking a lot, like when I stub my toe on the corner of my bed, when the internet goes out for a few seconds and the show I'm watching on Netflix pauses, and when a company chooses me as the person they want to hire out of all the other people they could have hired instead. Like, why me? I am never sure when it comes to the job thing, because there are most definitely other people out there who are better suited for these roles. There are for sure other people out there who are more impressive than me. But somehow the jobs were bestowed upon me. Yes, bestowed. Job offers are an honor.

It doesn't matter where or what the job is. If out of all the other people, they picked unexceptional you, that is an honor. Treat it as such. Then, remember this after you've been at your company for a while and want to start gossiping to your work friends about how much the people who hired you suck. They can't really suck that badly, right? They chose you. If anything, that at least means they're good enough at hiring.

3. Obtaining enough money to pay your bills.

Even if it's the only money I have at the moment, I have the money, and that's good enough for me (is it just me, or am I starting to sound like Cookie Monster?). Just call me Self-sufficient Sam because I can pay my bills. I am basically Beyoncé singing "Independent Woman." Except I didn't buy the house I live in. However, my hope is to one day be able to buy an average house to live in.

No matter what the bill is, whether it's a phone bill, a loan payment, a medical bill, a car payment, rent, or a mortgage, if you are paying something on a regular basis that is funding something important, you should be proud. I know, I know. Part of being an average human is paying bills. But if you weren't doing well, you wouldn't be able to. So, pat yourself on the fucking back for being good enough. You don't need to wait until you do something exceptional with your bill payments to recognize them.

4. Building a savings account.

When you're spending almost all of your paycheck on bills, groceries, and other important life expenses, it can be hard to imagine putting any of it away for you *not* to touch. If I could, I would go back to the very first time I ever received a paystub and start putting $15 a week into a savings account. If I had started doing this fifteen years ago and didn't touch the account until now, I would have well over $10,000 in it. All due to not spending $15 a week. That is literally not even equal to the amount of money I spend on coffee within a five-day period. That is insane.

See, a little bit *can* go a long way. A little bit is good enough. And so, if you are doing the bare minimum to save, that's good enough too. Just because you might not have as much money as experts say you should have saved at your age, be proud that at least you have something. Every bit counts. Revel in that.

5. Killing bugs on your own with no help.

Okay, so I am still afraid of bugs. But I've killed them on my own before, AND I WILL DO IT AGAIN. DO YOU HEAR THAT, SPIDERS? I AM A FIERCE, INDEPENDENT WOMAN WHO CAN KILL SPIDERS, thank you very much.

6. Calling the dentist to schedule appointments regularly.

I didn't go the dentist for five years because I kept putting off calling to make an appointment. That is actually nuts. For some reason, the small to-do's on my list never end and continue growing every day, so I kept overlooking a tiny thing like calling the dentist in favor of tasks that I would benefit from in that very moment. By the time I could internally justify prioritizing the "make dentist appointment" task on my list, my teeth were not pleased. That dentist appointment was pure hell. I had no cavities somehow, but I was there for, like, two hours while they scraped the shit out of my teeth. Just like I wish I did with my savings, I wish I had put aside the tiniest bit of time to schedule regular appointments during those five years I avoided the dentist. Then, I could have avoided the teeth scraping.

If you have a small task to do, whether it be scheduling a doctor's appointment, a haircut, a wax, a tan, whatever, remember to acknowledge the fact you did so. Tiny accomplishments matter. You don't have to put them off in favor of bigger, more impressive ones.

7. Keeping in touch with friends (even if you sometimes forget to respond to their texts).

You might not have the most friends, and you might not be the best friend, but if you have friends, that is really all that matters. After all, you don't have to be the best at something to be proud of the fact you did it. Having someone in your life who cares about you, whom you care for as well, is one of the most special things in this life. And every time you find such a special thing, you should celebrate it.

Sometimes I get into these moods where I feel like no one wants to hear from me, and so I don't reach out to anyone. Instead, I sit there thinking that I have no friends. But then I remind myself I do. It doesn't matter that I don't have an impressive number of them, and it doesn't matter that I don't have this exceptional social calendar where I see the friends I do have all the time. I have people I can reach out to. I have people who care about me. For that, I am lucky. Sure, like any average human, I can get too wrapped up in my own life. I forget to respond to texts. I say no to plans multiple weekends in a row. I go months without seeing certain people. But that doesn't mean I don't care. If someone told me they needed me, I would teleport there in an instant. I'm just kidding. I wish could teleport. But you get the point. People are not mind readers. Friendship takes effort, and as long as you're putting some amount of effort in, that's good enough. Go you.

8. Cooking dinner for yourself.

You know what? Fuck anyone who doesn't like when people post meals they cook to social media. This person did a thing, and they want to show it off. How is that any different from someone posting about the birth of a newborn child or a new job or an engagement? Okay, I realize those things are a little more serious than making the macaroni and cheese from Chrissy Teigen's cookbook, but what's so wrong with celebrating the small accomplishments that life brings?

We get so focused on only praising things that are *life-changing* that it can feel almost pathetic at times to be happy with mastering a simple feat. But let me tell you, it was a fucking triumph to learn how to cook a spaghetti squash, and it was a victory to find strength after a long day of work to cook chili over the stove. And if I chose to celebrate doing those things by taking a picture of my food while holding my desk lamp over it for lighting, so be it. We can celebrate however we damn please. Just as long as we're celebrating and not ignoring our little victories.

9. Doing things because you want to do them.

There is a certain joy not similar to any other joy that comes from being able to say NO to the shit you don't want to do and YES to the things you enjoy instead. Don't want to go to that party? Say no. Don't want to see that movie? Say no. Don't want to work in the field you're in anymore, but think you have to because your entire life has led to this? Say no to yourself and yes to trying out whatever you think you could love instead.

For too long, I said yes to plans that I didn't want to partake in, because I was afraid of missing out on an having an above-average social life. I went after a career I didn't end up loving, because I thought that's what I had to do in order to stand out from my peers. But while I was hard at work trying to impress others, I forgot about the person who matters most: me. Upon realizing nothing was coming from the things that didn't bring me joy, I stopped doing them. After this, I learned that no one cared that I didn't go to the party. No one thought I was a failure for changing my career path. In fact, no one cared except me. The only person you should aim to please in this life is yourself. If you do that, you'll please the people you care about *and* yourself at the same time. Everyone will win. And what do you do when you win? You celebrate!

10. *Being happy.*

The most important thing in this life to be proud of is your happiness. Real, legitimate happiness where you can't help but let it radiate off of your face into other people's lives. Smiles that are not fake. I know—smiles bring wrinkles and crow's feet with time. In fact, my mom told me point blank once that I have these things because I smile too much, and maybe that's true. But if that is the case, one can assume that my face is just celebrating my happiness. No, I am not always smiling, nor am I always happy. Sometimes I feel lonely. Sometimes I feel like a fraud. Sometimes I feel like a failure. Sometimes I feel unaccomplished. But in reality, I am none of those things. I mean, when I take into account all of the accomplishments above, I am a pretty decent human. Just because I'm not the most exceptional person I know doesn't mean I am doing something wrong.

My life, like so many, has had its ups and downs. Some of our lives have more intense ups, and others have more intense downs. Regardless, we are all out there living. We might as well find some happiness while doing it. And if you can find that gem of a feeling, if you can stop dwelling on the things you haven't done and the things that didn't go as planned, if you can stop comparing yourself to others, if you can stop feeling sorry about ending up "average," you'll smile. You might get a wrinkle or two while doing so, but wrinkles are average, and you are human. Ending up average doesn't mean you settled. Hell, *settling* doesn't mean you settled. It means you've found happiness with where you are right now. It doesn't mean you won't find more happiness in life. You will. But on your journey, as of right now, you're happy.

———

WHENEVER THE EMOTION arises, I now celebrate being happy. I might not be where I thought I'd be right now, and I might never get to some of the places I wanted to go, but fuck, I will try, and while I continue to make attempts—both failed and victorious—I will smile at the things I do accomplish along the way.

CONCLUSION

It's Okay to Do It Your Way

✦

HELLO! WELCOME! YOU have finally made it through this book! Congratulations! Another average accomplishment of which you can be supremely proud. Pat yourself on the back. Have a glass of wine. Take a nap. Watch another series on Netflix. I don't really care what you do to celebrate, as long as you acknowledge that yes, you are average—but because of that, you are also awesome as fuck.

TO SUM UP the book, let's go through all the reasons why.

Average does not mean awful.

IT DOES NOT mean you have failed, and it does not mean you are worthless. No, you might not become a billionaire one day. No, you might not become famous one day. No, you might not actually be skilled at the thing you thought you wanted to make a career out of one day. But you have a career. You have some money. You have a decent number of friends and family members.

Your life isn't what you pictured when you were in preschool and the teacher asked what everyone wanted to be when they grew up. But that's fine. Someone could have told you back then that your dreams were shit (my parents sure did, about becoming a cat and becoming famous, shout-out to my parents) to give you some padding for the hits you'd receive in the future, but most people were not told such things, and here we are.

Excellence can really be a straight-up hoax at times.

Maybe if kids grew up being taught to strive for the happy medium, we would not be here. Maybe if humans did not think of success only as reaching one's dream, they wouldn't feel like failures for not achieving them. Dreams happen when you're not awake, or they appear as holograms in your head. They are not real. Can dreams become real one day? Sure, maybe. But are you an awful person if they don't? No. You're just average. Normal. And you're doing just fine.

You don't have to be Beyoncé to do great things.

AVERAGE PEOPLE ACCOMPLISH shit, too. No, we might not be amazing at every little thing we do, but we do amazing little things every now and then. No, we're not perfect, but sometimes we have moments that feel perfect.

If you compare your life to the life of Beyoncé (or any influential person who is highly successful at multiple things), your life is going to seem not as good. That is science. But that doesn't mean your life is not good. You were just not born into the 1 percent of people who have extraordinary talents and the willpower to do literally anything to share those talents with the world. Case in point, you are normal.

But being normal doesn't mean you can't do great things. Maybe those things won't be great compared to what Beyoncé would do instead (you never know), but they can be great to you. And to be honest, that's really all that matters.

Sometimes, it's better to be ordinary than extraordinary.

EXCELLENCE CAN REALLY be a straight-up hoax at times. For starters, success comes with a whole bunch of responsibilities. It's the whole mo' money, mo' problems thing. If you have more money, you have more shit to deal with, whether that's the work stuff you're being paid the large sum of money to do, or the tax stuff you have to deal with in order to not fuck up the whole having-money thing, or the fighting off of estranged relatives who come out of the woodwork when one wins the lottery (I assume this is always what happens when someone wins the lottery).

And it's not just money. Extraordinary people tend to do crazy shit like wake up at 4 a.m. to start their days. No, thank you.

They stick to intense diets, leaving barely any wiggle room for things like pizza and french fries, in exchange for having impressive bodies. I'm all set.

They pay exorbitant amounts of money for personal trainers, who scream and yell until they are in shape. Yup, I'm good. I like going to barre class when I want to and sitting on the couch when I do not.

If they are famous, they can't leave their fucking homes without an entourage of people. Like, imagine not being able to go to Target alone on a Saturday morning to freely run around doing shopping cart drive-bys of the home décor section while adding and removing things from said cart without anyone noticing. If you're famous, they're going to fucking notice. Not that you'd be able to partake in this activity anyway, because you'd be *too* extraordinary.

Being average means you can do as you please without being held to any extraordinary expectations. You can just do you. And it's okay.

**Knowing you're not special motivates you
to work that much harder for exceptional moments.**

WHEN YOU THINK you're important, you expect things to
be handed to you. But when you know you're not special,
you're more likely to work for the things you want.

You won't complain about your job, wondering why
you're not being promoted for simply showing up to work
every day and doing the things you're asked to do. You'll ask
for that fucking promotion if you *really* did some extraordinary things and think you deserve it, and you'll understand
that it's okay if you don't get it. You have a good-enough
situation right now. You'll get there eventually.

You won't sit around your home, wondering why you
feel like you have no friends and why you're not making any
new connections. You'll put yourself out into the world and
be satisfied that you tried, no matter what happens.

You understand that you're just an ordinary person living an ordinary life in an ordinary world, and if you want to
break free from mundane moments, you better work (bitch;
sorry, the Britney fan in me couldn't help myself).

**Success is that much better when you
have embraced your mediocrity.**

IF YOU LIVE an entire life full of extraordinary moments, what
makes them special? What makes each of those moments
stand out from the others when they are all the same? To

have ups, you need to have downs. Picture a chart. If there are no lows, nothing would be high. Everything would just fall flat. And what is fun about a life that falls flat?

Success is not about how you appear to other people. Sure, it must be nice to know you seem impressive to other people, but what does that matter if you don't feel impressive to yourself?

Let's take Taylor Swift, for example. She knows she lives an extraordinary life. She knows she's above average in a world full of peasants. But do you think homegirl is out there making records that are just as good as her past ones, but not better? Or do you think she's always striving for more? Her bar of mediocre is so much higher than all of ours, meaning when she does something we commoners deem as successful she probably thinks it's shit.

Now, do I know this for a fact? Absolutely not. But one can assume success does not make her as happy anymore compared to how happy success makes us feel.

Another analogy: Here in New England (hi, haters), as you know, we win championships. A lot of championships, actually. (If you are putting away this book right now, I would like to take this time to say thank you for reading and goodbye.) I can tell you firsthand that the victory has gotten less sweet with time, but it is still sweet nonetheless. Winning games is our average over here. Like, some teams celebrate the fact they made it to the Super Bowl, even if they lose, and some (many) Patriots fans get angry when they make it to the Super Bowl and don't win. I'm not saying that I'd like to go back to the days when championship banners were few and far between in Boston, but I'm also saying that success is more exciting during the first parade than the five hundredth. Still just as fun, just less thrilling.

> **Praise is that much better, too, when you don't expect it for doing good-enough jobs.**

TO BE AVERAGE is to be good enough. To be average is also to know that good enough is exactly what's expected of you and nothing more.

If you do a good-enough job at something, why would you expect people to celebrate you for it? Weren't you expected to do a good-enough job on that thing? Isn't that why you were hired or asked to do it? Why are you presuming that you should be praised for the simple act of being an employee, parent, spouse, or friend? Why are you obsessed with outdoing yourself on all of these things at all times to impress people?

If you do an extraordinary job on something, sure, you might get recognition for going above and beyond expectations. But that shouldn't be something you are always striving for. Instead, you should aim for good enough and be pleased if you exceed your own expectations along the way. It's like the new "hope for the best and expect the worst." Hope for great, but expect (and accept) good enough.

Average is literally different for everyone, meaning all of this shit is yours to define, anyway.

BEING AVERAGE MEANS you're common. You're like everyone else. But everyone is different. So, doesn't that mean that being average is also being different? And, if so, doesn't that make your own average, whatever it may be, unique?

The answer: yes.

Like we discussed, Taylor Swift's average is different than yours. Beyoncé's average is different than yours too. I'm going to go out on a limb here and say that Taylor Swift's and Beyoncé's ideas of average are different from one another, too.

No matter who you are, your idea of average is based on your own perceptions of yourself against the world. But not everything is as it seems. And not everything will appear the same to everyone else. That's why you need to only consider yourself when defining average, because, after all, it's yours to establish.

Your average should be the norm. It should be the happy medium you strive for every day between wild success and minimal achievements. It should include achievements, but leave the big ones out for you to work toward. It should never be perceived as not good enough, because it *is* good enough. *You* are good enough. The next time your mind tries to tell you otherwise, remind yourself of that.

SO, WHAT *EXACTLY* have we learned here?

Average is not awful.

Success can be a burden.

Average is actually pretty damn good.

Thank you, love you, bye.

ACKNOWLEDGMENTS

First, I need to thank everyone who has walked into my life and made an impression while there. Good or bad, there would be no words or stories without you. To those mentioned in the book (you know who you are), thank you for whatever you did. I am eternally grateful.

Thank you to my extraordinary editor, Laura Mazer, for your guidance, vision, and support through this entire process. Without your brilliance, this book would be below average—extra ordinary at best. Thank you to the rest of the team at Seal Press and Hachette, as well.

None of this would have happened if my exceptional agent, Erin Niumata, did not take a chance on a young writer with an average social media following. Thank you for doing so and for helping me land the deal of my dreams. Also, thank you to Cristina Lupo for being an above-average assistant and finding my original manuscript in a pile of slush, reading it, and telling Erin she had to read it, too. I am indebted to your discovery.

My life would not be interesting to read about if it were not for my wonderful friends. Thank you to each and every one of you for making my life that much brighter and for still being here even though I was subpar at basic friend shit while writing this book. Special shout-out to my friends and coworkers who were forced into sharing their thoughts after I made them read unedited drafts of this. Their support kept me going. One day I will buy each of them an island. Just kidding. But we can pretend.

Thank you to my brothers for pretending to be excited about reading this book. In case you have actually made it to this page, hi. Tyler, thank you for always being there—and for not trying to one-up me on this accomplishment by writing your own book. Josh, thank you for continuously pushing me to do something big. Nick, thank you for enjoying one of the first stories I wrote (an *Entourage* spec script) and subsequently giving me confidence to write more. Also, you were eight. What the fuck?

I owe my writing skills to my mother, Jodi, who rewrote all of my papers in high school. If she had not forced me to read all of the tracked changes after doing so, I would probably not be able to form a sentence today. Thank you, Mom, for making me smarter, for giving me confidence, and for being my best friend. To my dad, Bill, I owe my weird sense of humor. Thank you for teaching me to not take life too seriously. Also, now you can stop telling me that I should go to law school. I love you all.

Thank you to my above-average husband, Dan, for putting up with me all these years and for letting me share our journey with the world. Without your incredible support, encouragement, and dinner decisions, this book would not exist. Thank you for believing in me when no one else did. I love you more than words.

And, finally, thank you to every single person who has read, shared, and followed my journey on the website ForeverTwentySomethings.com and the Instagram account @20somethingproblems over the years. I could not and would not have done this without you. You guys are the real MVPs.

Until next time . . .

MELISSA RORECH

Samantha Matt is the founder and editor in chief of ForeverTwentySomethings.com and runs the popular Instagram account @20somethingproblems. She is currently the director of audience development at Reviewed, a *USA Today* website, and her writing has appeared in *Women's Health, Cosmopolitan, Seventeen, Good Housekeeping, HuffPost,* and more. Samantha grew up in Canton, Massachusetts, a suburb of Boston, and graduated from Ithaca College in New York. She lives in Brookline, Massachusetts, with her husband and an unnecessary amount of clothes.